STUDYING DISASTER MOVIES

ALSO AVAILABLE IN THIS SERIES

Studying American Beauty

Jeremy Points

Studying Blade Runner

Sean Redmond

Studying Chungking Express

Sean Redmond

Studying City of God

Stephanie Muir

Studying The Matrix

Anna Dawson

Studying Surrealist and Fantasy Cinema

Neil Coombs

FORTHCOMING

Studying Alien

Elaine Scarratt

Studying Bollywood

Garret Fay

Studying Brokeback Mountain

James Clarke

Studying The Devil's Backbone

James Rose

Studying Tsotsi

Judith Gunn

STUDYING DISASTER MOVIES

John Sanders

John Sanders

is Head of Film Studies at Bedford Modern School, and the author of
The Film Genre Book (Auteur, 2009)

Dedication

For Dolores Tighe Sanders, my mother – a great survivor.

First published in 2009 by
Auteur, The Old Surgery, 9 Pulford Road, Leighton Buzzard LU7 1AB
www.auteur.co.uk
Copyright © Auteur 2009

Series design: Nikki Hamlett
Cover image *Cloverfield* © BFI Stills, Posters and Design
Set by AMP Ltd, Dunstable, Bedfordshire
Printed and bound in Poland; produced by Polskabook

British Library Cataloguing-in-Publication Data
A catalogue record for this book is available from the British Library

ISBN 978-1-903663-99-8

Contents

Introduction 7

1. A Brief History of the Disaster Film 9

2. Case Study 1 – *Airport* 21

3. Case Study 2 – *The Towering Inferno* 42

4. Case Study 3 – *The Day after Tomorrow* 67

5. Case Study 4 – *Cloverfield* 90

6. Parody and Reality – *Airport!* and *United 93* 112

Appendix: Creating your own Disaster Film 133

Spellbound

Emily Brontë

The night is darkening round me,
The wild winds coldly blow;
But a tyrant spell has bound me
And I cannot, cannot go.

The giant trees are bending
Their bare thoughts weighed with snow.
And the storm is fast descending,
And yet I cannot go.

Clouds beyond clouds above me,
Wastes beyond wastes below;
But nothing drear can move me;
I will not, cannot go.

Introduction

The twenty-first century and disaster... intimate bedfellows. The tone was set by 9/11, and the instant dissemination of information across the globe through news agencies, domestic digital cameras, mobile phones and the internet. It was my generation's JFK assassination moment. I sat on a train from St. Albans to Bedford, the journey punctuated by familiar sounds and stations. As I continued my progress northwards the first muted exclamations drifted towards me with passengers becoming unusually animated, confused and even a little exhilarated. The sounds of the train drained away as I started to feel excluded from something, a knowledge, an enlightenment which seemed to bring expressions of incomprehension, commuters shaken from their myopic reveries.

Then it was my turn. My mobile phone rang and a voice spoke of incredible and dastardly deeds. Even as I listened it sounded like the plot to a high-concept disaster film, only more outrageous than anything ever conceived before. My words of disbelief chimed with the chorus of voices in the carriage and my physical journey became an emotional one, a sense of unease seeping into my bones, something that has never really left me from that moment.

As the decade has progressed the world seems to have become beset by ever-more cataclysmic events. It is, in many ways, no different from previous decades but our access to these events has been made easy through the proliferation of new media technologies, and we can relive eyewitness visual and audio testaments time and again. We have intimate knowledge of what it is to live through a disaster; as I write the people of Burma are struggling to cope with the devastating effects of a cyclone and the Chinese have been plunged into a nightmarish world after an earthquake struck the Sichuan province. There are daily news bulletins about rising petrol prices, falling house prices, the 'credit crunch', spiralling street crime, the wars in Afghanistan and Iraq, and never too far away are the panics of a flu pandemic and terrorism.

In short, never has there been a better time for makers of disaster films! Global audiences are now served up the minutiae of people's suffering and miraculous survival. Images captured on mobiles and camcorders are fragments of first-hand personal records of disasters throughout the world, forming a tsunami of grainy, blurred, shaky video clips. Every disaster film cliché is seen for real, and we either turn away or, more often, are transfixed.

Cloverfield (2007) is the big screen manifestation – and culmination – of all these fragments. It has been a long filmic journey to reach this close-up portrait of destruction, but as Chapter 1 will detail, Hollywood has thrived on disaster from the very beginnings of film-making...

Chapter 1 – A Brief History of the Disaster Film

Disaster, or the impending threat of it, has always been an important element of films; there's nothing like someone else's dramatic misfortune to make an audience feel safe and secure. Many early films contained disaster elements, and the silent period is littered with moments of high drama as people fell prey to the elements. Biblical epics had the necessary disaster narrative conventions, with films such as Michael Curtiz' *Noah's Ark* (1928) containing scenes of peril that would become a staple for the disaster film genre. Other early disaster film templates include *The Last Days of Pompeii* (1913), *Metropolis* (1927) and *The Wind* (1928); although not fully realised disaster films they had elements or scenes that would reappear in later films.

The 1930s was not replete with disaster films, although there were a number that contained a catastrophic natural disaster as the narrative's denouement, such as Woody van Dyke's *San Francisco* (1936), John Ford's *The Hurricane* (1937) and Henry King's *In Old Chicago* (1937). If, of course, one looks at the staple B-movie genre of this decade, the Western, it is easy to discern the familiar disaster narrative of a group in peril reworked over and over again. The genre classic *Stagecoach* (1939) presents the disaster scenario of a disparate band of characters continually threatened by Native Americans, Hollywood's first generation of bad guys, later to be replaced by the extra-terrestrial fiends of sci-fi disaster films like *Independence Day* (1996) and *War of the Worlds* (2005).

The films of the 1940s were more concerned with one particular man-made 'disaster', the Second World War, while the following decade would see the rise of the science fiction film, the conventions of which are similar to those of the disaster film. A spate of films dealing with the destruction of humanity arose after the dropping of the atomic bombs in Hiroshima and Nagasaki at the end of the Second World War; films like Gordon Douglas' *Them!* (1954) detail how the nuclear age might create mutant creations (here, giant ants) that could annihilate civilisation. It was this sort of incredible and fictional terror that dominated the 1950s, just as people feared the unknown side effects of dabbling with the atom.

There were some films that certainly looked more like the disaster film that we recognise today in their dealings with 'real' situations where an ensemble cast of stars are subjected to either a natural or man-made disaster. William A. Wellman's *The High and the Mighty* (1954) charts the fate of 22 crew and passengers aboard a flight from Honolulu to San Francisco during which the plane suffers mechanical problems. The latter part of the film is true disaster territory, although the extended early flashback scenes to introduce the characters would be eschewed by later examples, which get to the action much earlier in the narrative. The 1957 film, *Zero Hour!*, would also be an influence on later disaster films with its story of food poisoning aboard a plane, not least the great parody of the plane disaster film, *Airplane!* (1980).

Maritime disasters and the sinking of the Titanic would also begin to fuel disaster films; the 1950s would see the release of two films based on the ocean liner's fate with *Titanic* (1953) and *A Night to Remember* (1958) initiating a series of productions that signalled film-makers' fascination with disasters at sea. These films were soon followed by *The Last Voyage* (1960) recounting a fictitious ship's final hours. The 1960s did not see a flowering of the genre, although there were some exceptions, notably a television film, *The Doomsday Flight* (1966), a precursor to many similar television films that reworked the 'flight-in-peril' narrative many times.

But it was not until the 1970s that the disaster genre, as we know it, was truly born. *Airport* (1970) set the tone and the template for this flowering of filmic mass destruction, positing the disaster centre stage and gleefully terrorising an array of famous names. With *Airport* the genre came of age, generating a massive financial return for its makers and even garnering a degree of critical acclaim and 10 Academy Award nominations. It seems appropriate that a decade which would usher in an era of global economic problems, an unpopular and seemingly unwinnable war, the ongoing Cold War and manifold evidence of political corruption should form the backdrop to a series of films with disaster at the heart of their narratives.

Timeline of disaster films or films with some disaster film conventions, 1910–1969

The Last Days of Pompeii (1913)

Noah's Ark (1928)

The Wind (1928)

La Fin Du Monde (1931)

The Last Days of Pompeii (1935)

San Francisco (1936)

The Hurricane (1937)

The Good Earth (1937)

In Old Chicago (1938)

The Rains Came (1939)

Titanic (1943, Ger.)

Titanic (1953)

A Night to Remember (1958)

Green Dolphin Street (1947)

Five (1951)

No Highway in the Sky (1951)

When Worlds Collide (1951)

The High and the Mighty (1954)

The Day the World Ended (1956)

A Night to Remember (1958)

On the Beach (1959)

The World, The Flesh, and the Devil (1959)

The Last Voyage (1960)

The Day the Earth Caught Fire (1961)

Fail-Safe (1964)

Crack in the World (1965)

Krakatoa, East of Java (1969)

The 27 films listed above are certainly not all disaster films – indeed, some of them are more rightly labelled as science fiction – but they all have elements of threat to humanity. For a 59-year period the number of films is extremely low, especially when compared with the 1970s alone. Over a 10-year-period there would be 24 disaster films:

Timeline of disaster films or films with some disaster film conventions, 1970–1979

Airport (1970)

Colossus: The Forbin Project (1970)

The Andromeda Strain (1971)

The Poseidon Adventure (1972)

Skyjacked (1972)

The Neptune Factor (1973)

Airport 1975 (1974)

Juggernaut (1974)

The Towering Inferno (1974)

Earthquake (1974)

The Hindenburg (1975)

Two-Minute Warning (1976)

Airport '77 (1977)

Black Sunday (1977)

Rollercoaster (1977)

Avalanche (1978)

City on Fire (1978)

Gray Lady Down (1978)

The Medusa Touch (1978)

The Swarm (1978)

Airport '79: Concorde (1979)

The China Syndrome (1979)

Meteor (1979)

Beyond the Poseidon Adventure (1979)

In contrast, the 1980s were quiet, perhaps precisely because there had been so much activity in the genre during the previous decade; it had seen a spectacular burst of destructive creativity and like many an explosion, volcano or killer bees the genre soon became exhausted. Irwin Allen, master of the genre and creative force behind two of the most popular and successful disaster films, *The Poseidon Adventure* and *The Towering Inferno*, directed *The Swarm* and *Beyond the Poseidon Adventure* at the end of the 1970s to critical derision and public indifference.

Not only were the major disaster films falling from grace but they were spawning a series of lacklustre cheap imitations; audiences, once stung, were twice shy about seeing another insect offering from 1978, *The Bees*. For the moment, the genre was in the doldrums and it would take 10 years and the explosion of computer generated imagery (CGI) technology before it became reinvigorated.

There *were* a few disaster offerings in the 1980s but these were generally under-funded and poorly received by critics and audiences alike. Irwin Allen's *When Time Ran Out...* (1980) was his final foray into theatrically-released features and it met with appalling reviews and suffered huge financial losses, damaging the genre's credibility even further. If Allen, the most potent force behind the modern disaster film, could not entice audiences to see his films, then it seemed the genre would struggle. Apart from a mere handful, notably *Virus* (1980), *The Quiet Earth* (1985) and *Runaway Train* (1985) the genre seemed all but extinct.

The studios had been bitten by the summer blockbuster bug in 1975 with the success of *Jaws*. Although Steven Spielberg's film had elements of the disaster genre, it broke away from the lumbering and elephantine action and narratives of previous films, laden with superstars, and appealed to the new must-have audience demographic, the teenager and 20-something patron with money to spend on a night at the cinema. This trend was further popularised by the fast-paced adventures of Luke Skywalker and Indiana Jones, which seemed a long way from the middle-aged antics of Charlton Heston and Gene Hackman in *Earthquake* and *The Poseidon Adventure* respectively.

In 1993 CGI came of age. *Jurassic Park* demonstrated its full capabilities by harnessing it to narrative drive and thereby heralding new possibilities for the return of the disaster film. Spielberg's film itself is part-disaster film, but its true reincarnation came with films like the true life account of Apollo 13's mission in Ron Howard's *Apollo 13* (1995), a *Poseidon Adventure* in space; *Outbreak* (1995); *Independence Day* (1996); *Twister* (1996); *Speed 2: Cruise Control* (1997); *Titanic* (1997); *Dante's Peak* (1997); *Volcano* (1997); *Deep Impact* (1997); *Armageddon* (1998) and *Godzilla* (1998).

Although these hybrid films cover such genres as action and science fiction, the disaster genre thread runs through them all. The plethora of disaster films in the 1990s has continued unabated into the new millennium; more advanced CGI technologies have opened up new visual possibilities for film-makers in this genre, and there has been a tendency for the disaster film to focus on global catastrophe rather than localised incidents. Films such as *28 Days Later* (2002), *The Core* (2003), *The Day After Tomorrow* (2004), *War of the Worlds* (2005), *Children of Men* (2006), *I Am Legend* (2007), *Sunshine* (2007), *28 Weeks Later* (2007) and *The Happening* (2008) all focus on the annihilation of humanity. Again, the genre has continued to cross-fertilise with the science-fiction, horror and action genres, drawing heavily on current fears, such as global warming, the threat of a flu pandemic, and that perennial favourite, nuclear oblivion.

The genre has also continued its penchant for re-enactment of real disasters. Although James Cameron looked back far into the century for the retelling of the infamous 1912 disaster in *Titanic* (1997), film-makers have increasingly begun to use recent history for inspiration; both Oliver Stone and Paul Greengrass tackled the 9/11 events in *World Trade Center* (2006) and *United 93* (2006) respectively. Even before these films had been released this event had become so well-documented that it already seemed to play like a film in people's minds, the haunting images and voices of the victims seen and heard by audiences across the globe.

In spite of this focus on disaster-fact rather than fiction, there were still a number of films that breathed the same old-fashioned air of the disaster films from the 1970s: *Poseidon* (2006) explicitly referenced the earlier film, although critical reaction was fairly indifferent and audiences were not particularly impressed; and *Snakes on a Plane* (2006) provided audiences with a novel twist on the *Airport*-style disaster film.

However, the genre has clearly mutated over the years and it seems that a straightforward disaster premise is no longer enough to guarantee a success. Out of the four films released in 2006 only *United 93* emerged as a clear critical success, and while it turned in a good profit on the relatively modest budget of $15,000,000, the film is not especially well-known, particularly amongst the younger film-goers unexcited by its low-key and unsensational approach to the storyline. Indeed, none of the other three films were critical successes and their financial returns were disappointing. *World Trade Center* demonstrated that an overly sentimental approach to recent real-life events was not universally popular, while *Poseidon* revealed that old formula disaster films updated with CGI effects were not necessarily improved. Meanwhile, *Snakes on a Plane* did not live up to its internet hype with a B-movie approach to the genre, a replay of the late 1970s with numerous low-budget, and inferior, imitators of the box office smashes.

So, where does the disaster genre go from here? As long as apocalyptic predictions about the world continue to interest both film-makers and audiences alike, filmic representations of the world's demise will surely continue. But what have been the disaster film's defining codes and conventions which made it so popular in the 1970s, and which have metamorphosed in recent years to create hybrid films where disaster is more of an element of the film's narrative thrust rather than the whole picture?

Codes and Conventions – Defining Disaster

In the 1970s the disaster film emerged in its strongest form, daring to become an established genre in its own right. But it is a magpie film type that has increasingly stolen from the science fiction genre to maintain its appeal. It is the child of the action/adventure genre, but takes on many different forms. It is a shape-shifting genre that now hides behind many other filmic facades; 1997 produced two disaster films that, on the outside, are very different: *Titanic* and Deep *Impact* inhabit different worlds but breathe the same disaster air.

Indeed, the disaster genre is a slippery beast and the full gamut of scenarios is extensive. Typical disaster narratives focus on natural disasters, accidents (caused either by a freak event or aided by human folly), terrorist or criminal attacks/plots, threats from space (either natural or by aliens) or they are technology-orientated (nuclear, computers, science). As such, the disaster film is able to tap into prevailing fears in any particular era and, indeed, appeal to the human fascination with people in peril; the rubbernecking motorist, craning to catch a glimpse of the car crash at the side of the road, is that evening's disaster film viewer.

The disaster film, then, is characterised by the following codes and conventions:

- A scenario where the normal equilibrium of life is disrupted by unusual and violent events.

- A hero or heroes who manage to overcome the disaster and save a small group of people (although the hero may die in the process).

- Characters from a range of backgrounds and with widely different personalities will often be thrown together by circumstance, and their interaction/conflict will be key to the narrative.

- Often a child or children will be present to add to the drama of the narrative.

- There will be an opening section where the key characters are sketched in and the disaster scenario is foreshadowed.

- The cause of the disaster can often be sourced back to man's incompetence, meddling or hubris; even if it is not down to these factors, man's reaction to the disaster is shown to be flawed.

- The initial impact of the disaster will result in the death of many people, leaving the narrative to focus on a small group.

- Even characters in the focus group will be killed during the narrative.

- There will be a series of obstacles which the focus group must overcome to reach safety.

- Villains/unpleasant characters will eventually be killed, but the more sympathetic characters are not immune from death.

- There will be episodes where good characters will sacrifice themselves for the survival of the group.

- There will often be a romantic attachment between two characters.

- The disaster will either run its natural course and subside, or the main protagonist/s (usually an unsung professional person who has more common sense than all the world leaders/politicians/military put together) will manage to execute a spectacular rescue or solve the conundrum of how to avert a cataclysmic disaster.

- As most disaster films are Hollywood-made, the United States is often the scene of the disaster and its individuals/armed forces will often save the day.

- The emphasis will be on spectacularly destructive events, tension and human drama throughout the film.

- There will often be a well-known cast affording an audience with the pleasure of guessing who will be the next victim.

- There will often be a moral, a lesson to be learned by individuals or humanity at the end of the film.

Disaster films will exhibit some or all of these conventions, and as we have seen, they will appear dressed up in a number of different genres. Certainly, there seems to have been a shift from the domestic or localised situation (*The Towering Inferno*; *The Poseidon Adventure*) to the universal and cataclysmic (*Armageddon*; *The Day After Tomorrow*), perhaps reflecting an increasingly anxious world.

As a way of examining the genre's codes and conventions it is now important to look at some disaster films in detail, using each one to tease out the common and less common strands that define the genre.

Chapter 2: Case Study 1 – *Airport*

KEY FACTS

Release Date: 1970

Country of Origin: USA

Running Time: 137 minutes

Budget

$10,000,000 (estimated)

Marketing – Tagline

The best seller that is now a great motion picture...

PRODUCTION NOTES

Production Company

Universal Pictures

Distributor

Universal Pictures

The tagline references the novel by Arthur Hailey, an incredibly successful book published in 1968, and selling millions of copies around the world. In this way the tagline explicitly connects the film with success and popularity that the producers hope will transfer to box office triumph, which indeed is exactly what happened. Also, linking the film to such a worldwide publishing phenomenon gives the film a built-in audience eager to see a favourite book transferred onto the screen.

Posters

This US one-sheet poster focuses on the stars involved in the film; it is an all-star cast, the sort that would have only been seen in blockbuster films such as the war film, *The Great Escape* (1963) or the biblical epic, *The Greatest Story Ever Told* (1965). It was unusual for films with a more domestic setting to have such big all-star casts, although there were exceptions, such as *Grand Hotel* (1932), which used a similar strategy in its poster campaign (see opposite).

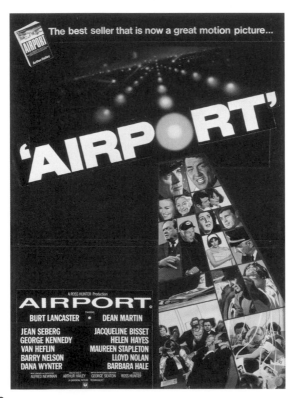

The *Airport* poster is dominated by photographs of its stars, emphasising their importance to the marketing process and helping the audience identify with big star names. Burt Lancaster and Dean Martin were certainly very well-known actors of the time, who had been active in Hollywood from the 1940s (Lancaster) and 1950s (Martin) onwards. The other stars would have ensured that the film was attractive to a wide range of ages: Jacqueline Bisset was an up and coming English actress who had starred alongside Steve McQueen in the incredibly popular and stylish police thriller, *Bullitt*, two years earlier; Jean Seberg had made a striking impression on audiences in her early films, notably *Saint Joan* (1957), *Bonjour Tristesse* (1958) and *Breathless* (1959); Helen Hayes' film career traced back to 1917 and she remained a popular star of film and, especially, stage; and Lloyd Nolan's screen credits began in the 1930s. Indeed, there was something, or someone, for everyone in this film and the poster plays on this fact.

The other notable aspect of the poster is that it features a picture of the novel upon which the film is based, further cementing the film's connection with the bestselling book.

Trailer

The film trailer, like the posters, emphasises the film's link to the novel and its all-star cast; it actually says that it has 'the biggest all-star cast ever assembled for a Universal motion picture'. Initially, we see the novel superimposed onto an aircraft's landing gear and then there are portraits of the cast. The emphasis is on 'big', a word used a number of times in the voice-over, the all-American male tone giving the narration a dramatic edge. At the beginning of the trailer the orchestral score is also suitably strident with its surging brass section over scenes from the film.

There is further emphasis on the film's connection with the novel as it shows images of the book translated into numerous languages, underlining its worldwide appeal. The suggestion is that if the book was fantastic then so the film must be too. The narration also talks of 'Academy award-winning George Seaton'; this connection with the Oscars was, and is, a very important marketing point for films (Seaton had previously won two Oscars for his screenplays of *Miracle on 34th Street* (1947) and *The Country Girl* (1954)). The section where the seven threads of the narrative are shown forms the main body of the trailer with fairly long sequences (the trailer is edited at a much slower pace than would be expected today), and the voice-over reiterating the star power that is involved.

Next, some dramatic images are shown (related to the film's finale) and the dramatic music returns, making the visuals more impressive. The voice-over underlines the film's epic scale with the repetition of the line '*Airport* has no equal' and the final image, where the plane plummets into the darkness and the clouds, is designed to leave the audience in no doubt that this will be a thrilling and spectacular film.

Synopsis

The Lincoln International Airport is beset by a number of problems during a snowy night in winter. Initially, a landing plane comes off the runway and gets stuck in the snow. This is the beginning of a chaotic night for the airport's manager and his staff. An elderly stowaway is found on a flight, a local resident threatens the airport with legal action, and a disturbed and impoverished man takes a homemade bomb onto a flight, which he intends to detonate so that his wife will collect the insurance money.

This main thread of the narrative is interwoven with the background stories of the main characters: the friction between the airport manager and his wife, as well as an affair between the threatened plane's pilot and an English flight attendant, who is pregnant with his child. Ultimately, the bomber blows himself up and is sucked out of the plane's toilet window, the blast injuring the English flight attendant and endangering all the passengers with the sudden decompression of the interior. In spite of the blizzard and the damage to the aircraft, the pilots manage to land the plane safely and without any major injuries.

Commentary

In the voice-over narration for the film's trailer one of the elements that is emphasised is the use and size of a very well-known cast, demonstrating the scale of the film. As with other disaster films to come in the 1970s it sets up back stories for each of the main characters and eventually interweaves their stories so that the audience can identify with them when disaster strikes. This use of an ensemble cast and interlinking narratives was not new; such early films as Edmund Goulding's *Grand Hotel* (1932), winner of the Academy Award for Best Picture, charts the lives of a wide range of characters, all united at the eponymous establishment, but without the disaster finale.

Airport's budget of approximately $10,000,000 was enormous for its time, compared with $2,200,000 and $3,500,000 for *Love Story* and *M*A*S*H*, the other highest earning films of that year. Indeed, its success puts the film at number 40 in the top 50 highest grossing films of all time when adjusted for inflation. Although there is only one death (the bomber) and any real disaster is averted, the film still remains an important template for the likes of *The Poseidon Adventure* two years later and *The Towering Inferno* in 1974. They would follow *Airport* with their stellar casts, high production values, big budgets, multiple strand plots, build-up of tension and the final disaster, or averted disaster. Where the later films diverged from *Airport* is in their casual disregard for the status of their stars by killing them off, and making for a more nail-biting experience for the audience, whose expectations were initially undermined by this tactic, but who came increasingly to expect the blood of stars to be spilled.

In many ways the film resembles a soap opera with its stories of illicit affairs and crisis scenarios, based as it is on popular writer Arthur Hailey's bestselling book. His novels, including *Hotel* and *Wheels*, tend to delve into the political manoeuvrings and private lives of those involved in large communities or corporations. The soap opera element is, of course, ripe for parody because of the melodramatic nature of the storylines.

By 1980, the disaster boom of the previous decade was in decline, and as with other genres when they run their course, it was ready for a parody of its often over-inflated codes and conventions. This came in the form of *Airplane!* (1980), which used *Airport* as its main target; the parody is very close to the original with a similarly dramatic score, the same basic narrative, reworking a number of the scenes (including the slapping of an hysterical passenger), the same camera set-ups for scenes (in the cockpit, for example) and even the same typeface for the opening titles.

Theme

Experts/expertise

Disaster films will always have at least one character who manages to overcome the challenges that beset a group of people or, indeed, a nation. In *Airport* there are a number of characters who use their expertise to face the challenges confronting them. The airport manager is the chief protagonist, whose personal and professional life is presented as a series of challenges. His socialite wife demands his attention, and on the night of the film's narrative he juggles a stranded plane, a blizzard, a stowaway, a possible law suit from a nearby resident over noise and disruption from the planes and the bomber on another aircraft. All this is handled with efficiency and determination.

It is not just the airport manager who is singled out; his assistant is calm and hardworking; the pilot of the threatened aircraft faces the challenges without a fuss; one stewardess is courageous; the engineer, Petroni, is level-headed and tough and one of the customs officials is shown to be intuitive throughout. Each of these characters is given one or more scenarios where their expertise is tested, but each succeeds, forming a unit of people who are dependable and resourceful.

Other disaster films present the same level of expertise, where characters who can perform under pressure come to the fore. The Steve McQueen chief of fire fighters in *The Towering Inferno* (1974) is a prime example, as are many of his men: he can fight fires, effect rescues whilst suspended on a winch from a helicopter *and* work effectively as an explosives expert. In *The Day After Tomorrow* (2004) it is the combined forces of the scientists who guide the response to the global catastrophe and who undertake the heroics of the film, a similar scenario to that of *Armageddon* (1998) where engineers save the day. It is not so much that they are always the absolute world authority on issues, but they are dedicated and professional in their own world; they operate beyond the corruption and incompetence often represented in establishment figures, eschewing words in favour of prompt and decisive action. With a coat of Hollywood gloss they all become everyday heroes, their purity of action distinguishing them from the masses whose salvation lies in the hands of the disaster films' gallery of experts.

SELECT FILMOGRAPHY OF MAIN PRODUCERS AND CAST

George Seaton, 1911–79, Director

Miracle on 34th Street, 1947
The Big Lift, 1950
The Country Girl, 1954
Teacher's Pet, 1958
36 Hours, 1965
Airport, 1970

Ross Hunter, 1920–96, Producer

All That Heaven Allows, 1955
Imitation of Life, 1959
Pillow Talk, 1959
Thoroughly Modern Millie, 1967
Airport, 1970

Burt Lancaster, 1913–1994, Actor

The Killers, 1946
From Here To Eternity, 1953
Apache, 1954
Gunfight at the O.K. Corral, 1957
Sweet Smell of Success, 1957
Run Silent, Run Deep, 1958
Elmer Gantry, 1960
Birdman of Alcatraz, 1962
The Leopard, 1963
Seven Days in May, 1964
The Train, 1964
The Professionals, 1966
The Swimmer, 1968
Airport, 1970

Ulzana's Raid, 1972
1900, 1976
The Cassandra Crossing, 1976
Twilight's Last Gleaming, 1977
Zulu Dawn, 1979
Atlantic City, 1980
Local Hero, 1983
The Osterman Weekend, 1983
Tough Guys, 1986
Field of Dreams, 1989

Dean Martin, 1917–95, Actor

Some Came Running, 1958
Rio Bravo, 1959
Ocean's Eleven, 1960
The Sons of Katie Elder, 1965
The Silencers, 1966
5 Card Stud, 1968
Airport, 1970
The Cannonball Run, 1981

REPRESENTATION

Airports

Airports were, and continue to be, places of both great excitement and anxiety. By 1970, when *Airport* was made, air travel had become relatively commonplace within the US, and the beginnings of mass tourism by package holiday was on the horizon in Europe. There is still something exhilarating and almost miraculous about air travel; although an extremely safe way to travel, plane crashes inevitably attract high levels of media attention. The anticipation of a holiday or visit to family and friends is also mixed with the fear of being trapped 30,000 feet up in the sky, hurtling through the atmosphere at tremendous speeds. These feelings, and the stress of negotiating the airport procedures and saying farewells/welcomes to travellers, add to the drama of the airport environment.

Hollywood has long realised the appeal of using airports/air travel as a backdrop to human drama, going as far back as 1939 in Howard Hawks' *Only Angels Have Wings*, which detailed the excitement and drama of air travel (in this case, freight planes in a South American country), and its effect on those waiting on the ground. Films that more specifically centre on life in an airport include *The V.I.P.s* (1963) and *The Terminal* (2004), whilst they play a significant part in films like *Planes, Trains and Automobiles* (1987) and *Die Hard 2: Die Harder* (1990). Whatever the genre, these films show airports as sites which generate a deep unease and, sometimes, absolute chaos.

Airport begins with a black screen, with just the cacophony of sound produced by the crowds at an airport; it signifies energy, controlled chaos and a community. The image that is finally revealed shows a mass of humanity, like swarming ants, all with their own individual story, but part of this migration. The airport is represented as a place where work continues regardless of weather conditions; it is an endless cycle of preparation and hard graft to keep the airport operating. The airport is shown to be run by a group of hardened veterans who can deal with any problem that is thrown at them: there is the tough airport manager, the maverick head mechanic, the all-seeing customs official, the heroic pilot and a whole range of supporting staff.

Audiences have been long fascinated with the machinations of airports and airlines, and indeed, in recent years they have watched the day-to-day lives of airports and their staffs in reality television programmes like *Airport* (UK, 1996-2008) and *Airline* (USA, 2004-2005). All these productions manage to convey the personal dramas that are played out each day in airports. Even Hollywood does not need to exaggerate too much, considering the real-life events that have affected airports and the aviation industry in recent years, particularly the threat and reality of terrorist attacks.

Actors

Burt Lancaster

Burt Lancaster was a very athletic leading actor from the 1940s; initially, he was an acrobat and then moved into film-making, first as an actor and then as a producer as well. He made a range of films from westerns to romances, and from film noir to comedies in a career spanning more than 40 years. He is notable for his intelligent performances in
serious films, often exploring notions of individual integrity and professionalism; films like *Apache* (1954), *Sweet Smell of Success* (1957), *Birdman of Alcatraz* (1962), *The Leopard* (1963), *The Train* (1964), *The Professionals* (1966) and *Ulzana's Raid* (1972) are mostly genre films but which transcend their genre conventions to explore a range of issues.

Dean Martin

Dean Martin was known as much for his singing as his acting during his career, and he seemed to bring his laconic public persona to all his acting roles. He was generally typecast as a good-humoured playboy, with a fondness for alcohol and women. He was part of Frank Sinatra's (in)famous Rat Pack, a group of high-living socialite actors  and singers who essentially portrayed exaggerations of themselves in classic Hollywood bad boy mode. Although Martin played up to this public persona and some of his roles seemed to be extensions of this (*The Silencers*, 1966, for example, as an incredibly laid-back James Bond character; an American Austin Powers), there were some roles in which his acting talents were displayed, particularly in Vincente Minnelli's *Some Came Running* (1958) and Howard Hawks' *Rio Bravo* (1959). It has to be said, however, that critics did find it difficult to take him seriously as the heroic airplane captain in *Airport*, when he seemed much better suited to the role of the alcoholic Dude in *Rio Bravo*.

TEXTUAL ANALYSIS

Bomb explosion (DVD chapter 13, 1:36:28)

Summary

The crew of the airplane have been told that there is a man with a bomb on board. They decide to use the old lady bedside him, who is a stowaway, in their plan to get the briefcase, containing the bomb, out of his grasp. The plan almost works but an interfering passenger disrupts proceedings and the bomber reclaims his briefcase. The pilot manages to convince him to hand over the case, but just as he is doing so a passenger emerges from the toilet behind him and he panics. Whilst in the toilet he detonates the bomb; he is sucked out of the hole, a stewardess is injured and the plane is forced to begin the descent to make an emergency landing.

Camerawork

The medium long shot of the plane's interior sets up the context for the action with the stowaway and stewardess centre frame as they will be the focus of the next piece of action. The pilot's POV shot adds a sense of mystery to the sequence; the audience has not heard the plan and will be wondering how the crew are going to foil the bomber. In order to maintain the tension, the next few shots both include and exclude the bomber; the audience is shown that he is ever-present but is denied a continuous look at his reactions to events. The attempt to take his briefcase is shown in a series of medium shots with some movement to add to the chaotic sequence.

When the bomber has escaped with his case there are a number of shots from behind him, framed against the crew and passengers, to demonstrate that he is alone and isolated, an outsider. These alternate with medium shots of the bomber, isolated in the widescreen frame. This latter shot contrasts with the next one, a medium shot of the crew and passengers, a tightly packed group, showing their solidarity against him.

Eventually, the pilot is reframed with the passengers seated behind him; again he looks part of a community, foregrounded to show his importance and heroic nature, with the support of many, whilst the bomber is on his own and without support. The framing gets closer on both the pilot and the bomber as their conversation continues, helping to underline the tension and intensity of the action. The shot of the bomber in the toilet again shows him alone in the frame, except for his own reflection in the mirror, prompting guilt and self-loathing, and he then opens the case.

The explosion is shown side-on, framing another stewardess and passenger in the foreground to show the effect on others and giving the action more impact. The next shot looks directly towards the hole created by the explosion; in this way the audience is placed in the position of the people and objects

that are being sucked towards the opening. The long shot of the passengers helps to emphasise the devastating effects of the sudden decompression, allowing as much chaos to be shown as possible, a shot that is repeated after a view of the pilots.

The tracking shot of the pilot's body, as he is dragged along the floor, re-connects the audience to the action. The following shot of the stewardess is taken from the direction of the hole and she is dragged towards us, positioning the audience directly in the midst of the chaos, and then there is another shot of the hole, emphasising the nature of the threat to all the passengers and the stewardess in particular. The final shots of passengers and then back to the damage help to show that the immediate danger is over.

Sound

There is only diegetic sound throughout this sequence, which helps to underline the reality of the action. In the opening violent exchange between stewardess and stowaway there is the general hum of the plane and the outraged murmur of the watching passengers, again underlining the verisimilitude of the scene. The cacophony of shouts during the struggle for the briefcase adds to the chaos of the action, and this is then contrasted with the pilot's calm and low-level voice as he tries

to pacify the bomber. Whilst the passenger emerges from the toilet and the bomber enters it, there is further shouting to underline the passengers' panic. This is followed by a moment in the toilet as the bomber contemplates his future with the sounds of tapping on the door and muted shouts from outside increasing his sense of being cornered. The muted sounds make the subsequent loud explosion all the more shocking.

It is unexpected and designed to surprise the audience whilst the sounds for rest of the scene, as the plane decompresses and plummets to earth, help to emphasise the sense of chaos. We hear the deafening sound of the whirling wind, the screams of the passengers, the creaking aircraft plunging through the sky and the warning beeps in the cockpit; all are devised to convey the feelings of terror and panic being felt by the passengers as they try to cope with the aftermath of the bomb blast.

By only using diegetic sound the audience is drawn into the action by the range of unsettling sounds in this edgy sequence, helping the tension build in a more natural manner without the need to be prompted by a musical score. The atmosphere created is one where the sound of the explosion is all the more unexpected as the audience is given no musical cues to suggest that the dramatic moment is about to happen. In this way the sequence, unlike other parts of the film, has less of the Hollywood gloss associated with spectacle films where dramatic moments are often underscored by an emphatic orchestral score.

Editing

The sequence follows the standard rules of continuity editing, so that the narrative unfolds to the audience in a coherent way. The pace of the editing is steady at the beginning of the sequence but increases in pace significantly as the struggle ensues and at the beginning of the conversation between pilot and bomber, highlighting the chaos and then the tension of the action. The cutting between pilot and bomber establishes a link between these two men; the passengers' safety seems to rest on this all-important interaction. There are then a couple of quick cuts when the bomber runs into the toilet and the stewardess runs to the door, underpinning the urgency of the action, and the subsequent shot runs for a few moments longer in order to make the explosion, which synchronises with the cut back to the stewardess outside, all the more unexpected and shocking. The cuts for the rest of this chaotic sequence are all fairly rapid, in keeping with the confusion of the scene, combining the pilot, the stewardess and the passengers in this moment of extreme danger.

Mise-en-scène

Character and performance

The long shot shows the inside of an airplane complete with seats, passengers and items in overhead shelves; it is a busy frame with ample possibilities for chaos to develop. The old lady, the stowaway, is held roughly by the stewardess, her head is bowed and her face registers anguish. This is the beginning of the dramatic episode that will unfold. The stewardess is, like the stowaway, playing a part (to fool the bomber) and she is upright and aggressive. The old lady is in black and she is short, adding to her vulnerability next to the more statuesque and young stewardess. All the passengers stare in the direction of the stewardess and the stowaway, their expressions of anger and surprise underlining the sense of mounting tension. The body language of the stewardess continues to be aggressive whilst the stowaway is pleading and defensive.

Most of the passengers are middle-aged and well-dressed, the sort of respectable people who would be outraged by the stewardess' actions. In the background there are two nuns, with their connotations of peace marking a direct contrast to the violent behaviour of the stewardess. Her aggressive action continues to be met with fear from the old lady and anger from the onlookers. Noticeably, only the bomber ignores these events, adding to the sense that his fear of exposure dominates his actions. The rest of the movement and gesture in the next few shots contains a slap and people fighting/

jostling, all of which adds to the general sense of chaos. The bomber is dressed in a sober black suit and his face is sweaty and worried-looking; he is an unappealing character, appropriate for a desperate man who is about to blow up the plane. In contrast, the pilot is smartly dressed in his grey uniform, the picture of a good-looking hero. As the two men talk, their expressions define their feelings; the pilot is earnest and honest, whilst the bomber is frightened and guilt-ridden. In the toilet cubicle the mirror dominates the mise-en-scène; the bomber sees his image and this adds to his sense of despair and then his resolve that he may as well kill himself as he has nothing to live for.

Once the explosion has taken place, the mise-en-scène is dominated by its chaotic aftermath. The neatly ordered rows of seats and stacked shelves are thrown into disarray with objects flying throughout the cabin in a scene of carnage and confusion. Clothes, like those of the stewardess caught in the explosion, are shredded by the decompression; everything and everyone is caught up in this nightmarish maelstrom. The poses and movements of all the passengers underline the danger; they are all in defensive postures, powerless to stop the forces of nature. The appearance of the oxygen masks is the end of the first part of the danger, the desperate and battered passengers gratefully grabbing them to bring some relief.

Colour and lighting

The dominant colours in the scene are the grey and yellow livery of the aircraft interior and the crew's uniforms, lending the scene an air of reality and normality; this contrasts with the mainly dark colours of the passengers, helping to define them as individuals against the neutral seats. Everything is brightly-lit (high-key lighting), to mirror the usual lighting of a plane's interior. The only characters who are afforded some shadow are the crew in the cockpit, investing it with a sense of safety, almost womb-like, and for the bomber when he stands facing the rest of the passengers and when he is in the toilet cubicle.

Once the explosion has taken place the lighting becomes less even, with patches of darkness as the passengers and crew struggle to cope with the effects of sudden decompression. In particular, the stewardess injured by the blast and twisted by the force of the wind as she lies on the floor, is shown in shadow to emphasise the danger of her predicament.

The shot of the damage caused by the explosion is darkly lit around the hole in the background, signifying its danger, a black hole trying to consume everyone and everything. Finally, when some control is restored and the oxygen masks appear the passengers are seen in an even light but it seems fainter than before, underlining the drains on their vitality. The darkness at the back of the plane where the explosion has occurred signifies the danger still stalking the passengers and crew.

'In the early 70s transport really wasn't safe in the movies. Planes, of course, crashed, but don't knock it - there's drama there, too... OK, it's hokey old stuff, but it's still gripping soap opera.' **FilmFour**

'The plot has few surprises (you know and I know that no airplane piloted by Dean Martin ever crashed). The gags are painfully simpleminded (a priest, pretending to cross himself, whacks a wise guy across the face). And the characters talk in regulation B-movie clichés... The movie has a lot of expensive stars, but only two (Helen Hayes and Van Heflin) have wit enough to abandon all pretence of seriousness... Heflin, as the guy with the bomb in his briefcase, is perhaps the only person in the cast to realize how... absurd *Airport* basically is. The airplane already has a priest, two nuns, three doctors, a stowaway, a customs officer's niece, a pregnant stewardess, two black GIs, a loudmouthed kid, a henpecked husband, and Dean Martin aboard, right? So obviously the bomber has to be typecast, too... What Heflin does is undermine the structure of the whole movie with a sort of subversive overacting. Once the bomber becomes ridiculous, the movie does, too.'
Roger Ebert, Jan 1 1970

Chapter 3: Case Study 2 – *The Towering Inferno*

KEY FACTS

Release Date: 1974

Country of Origin: USA

Running Time: 165 minutes

Budget

$14,000,000 (estimated)

PRODUCTION NOTES

Production Companies

Irwin Allen Productions

Warner Bros. Pictures

Fox Film Corporation

Distributors

Fox Film Corporation

Warner Bros. Pictures

Marketing – Taglines

One Tiny Spark Becomes A Night Of Blazing Suspense

A typically dramatic Hollywood tagline with the employment of a pun, using the words 'spark' and 'blazing' to connect with the fire theme.

The tallest building in the world is on fire. You are there with 294 other guests... There's no way down. There's no way out.

One minute you're attending a party atop the world's tallest skyscraper. The next... you're trapped with 294 other guests in the middle of a fiery hell.

The world's tallest building is on fire. You are there on the 135th floor... no way down... no way out.

All four of these taglines position the audience within the drama to make the message more effective and dramatic; it taps into a common and very real fear, that of being trapped in burning building, a daily news event.

Posters

Unusually for a film poster the background is in black; a colour that serves two functions: it is sombre, connoting death and in keeping with the dramatic tone of the film. Also, the white taglines on the poster stand out against the background as do the two other dominant colours, red and yellow, which, of course, connect with the fiery theme of the film.

Without an actual building (in the film it is a combination of model, matte painting and studio set) to include in the poster, a graphic illustration is used instead. This allows for a far more dramatic picture, an extension and elaboration of what we actually see on screen. This film, of course, was made in pre-CGI times and it was not possible to effectively recreate spectacular images from the film in poster art. Compare this with two other famous films from the 1970s, *Jaws* (1975) and *Star Wars* (1977), both of which are also illustrations rather than actual stills from the films which would have looked like miniatures or models, and therefore rather unrealistic.

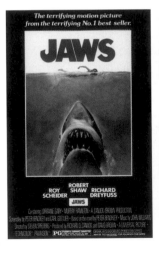

Taglines aside, the text for 'INFERNO', as with the film title sequence, is a mixture of yellow and red, and it is wavy, mimicking the appearance of a flame.

With so many stars in the film it was also important to indicate their presence and so there are two large photographs of 1970's superstars Steve McQueen and Paul Newman to attract audiences. It is interesting to note that McQueen appears on the left, just as his name does, and Newman is on the right, giving McQueen, in effect, the top billing. However, Newman's photograph and name are just above McQueen's, mirroring the opening titles of the film, almost balancing out the issue of who should be the top billed actor (see section on Steve McQueen).

The other main actors have their photographs as well; this was such a stellar cast that their involvement is a great publicity boon for the film. William Holden was the golden boy of Hollywood in the 1940s and he was particularly successful in the 1950s with romantic films such as *Sunset Boulevard* (1950), *Born Yesterday* (1950), *Sabrina* (1954), *Love Is A Many-Splendored Thing* (1955) and *Picnic* (1955), which he then consolidated by some more serious films, particularly *The Bridge On The River Kwai* (1957), *The Wild Bunch* (1969) and *Network* (1976). Faye Dunaway was the quintessential 1960's film star, part of a new breed of young females who played unconventional characters. She had made her name in films such as *Bonnie and Clyde* (1967), *The Thomas Crown Affair* (1968) and *Chinatown* (1974). Meanwhile, Fred Astaire had captivated cinema audiences between the 1930s and 1950s with a string of highly successful musicals, including *Top Hat* (1935), *Holiday Inn* (1942), *Easter Parade* (1948) and *The Band Wagon* (1953).

The presence of these stars would make the film attractive to a wide variety of audiences, not just a young demographic, who would naturally be drawn to an action film. Finally, each photograph carries a description of their character's role in the film (The Fire Chief, The Architect, etc.) which helps to broaden the relevance of the characters; it is a list of both VIPs and normal people, suggesting that everyone will get caught up in this nightmarish sequence of events.

Trailer

The trailer begins with an image of Steve McQueen and Paul Newman, reinforced by their names being used by the voice-over; they were the biggest superstars of their day and this is an important selling point for the film. Audiences had long anticipated their appearance together on screen. One of the opening lines in the trailer is 'one tiny spark becomes a night of blazing suspense', which attempts to create a sense of drama and the images are all moments of action and danger in order to make it clear that this is a nerve-shredding experience for the viewer.

The use of a dramatic orchestral score helps to underpin the sense of excitement and there is extensive use of siren noises and explosions to maintain the atmosphere of action and thrills. The names and images of the two main actors are then reiterated, along with the names of the other stars; this idea of the all-star cast is a fundamental part of the 1970's disaster film and provided a strong hook for audiences.

When the film's title appears on screen there are a number of synchronised explosions to give the moment more impact. There is also the use of images to show the relationships between characters, such as Paul Newman and Faye

Dunaway, to deepen the emotional impact of the trailer, and the voice-over continues to include emotive language. There is also reference to its producer, Irwin Allen, and his very popular disaster film, *The Poseidon Adventure*, made two years earlier, intended to underline *The Towering Inferno*'s pedigree. There is even a *third* mention of the two top billed stars in the film, so important are they to the film's appeal. The pace of editing is fairly rapid to reinforce the idea that this is a dynamic film. Towards the end it speeds up even more as it shows images of characters' faces as they wait for the final climatic explosion.

Synopsis

The glittering gala opening of the highest building in the world, the Glass Tower, is shattered by the outbreak of a fire below rooms where assembled VIP guests are celebrating. It soon becomes clear to the building's owner that his son-in-law, in charge of electricals for the building, has installed sub-standard wiring in order to keep costs down. Whilst the building is evacuated the party near the top of the skyscraper continues, until it is too late to escort them back down the building. As the fire creeps upwards the lifts fail, there are explosions as gas begins to leak and fire and the explosions destroy the stairwells. A number of rescue attempts are made, both by breeches' buoy and by helicopter, but they ultimately fail. Finally, the chief fire officer and the building's architect join forces to detonate some explosives next to huge water tanks at the top of the building. The plan works and water cascades down the building and extinguishes the flames. Some of the trapped guests die in the torrent of water but most survive, with the chief fire officer and his men emerging as the heroes.

Commentary

The success of the Irwin Allen-produced *The Poseidon Adventure* secured the funding for *The Towering Inferno* two years later. Allen's work on television had also been a great success, earning him the professional power to move into feature films. All his television productions, including *Voyage to the Bottom of the Sea* (1964–68), *Lost in Space* (1965–68), *The Time Tunnel* (1966–67) and *Land of the Giants* (1968–70), relied heavily on tension and action set-pieces, a solid grounding for his later work. His name became synonymous with the disaster genre during the 1970s and he became known as the 'Master of Disaster', making huge amounts of money for the studios involved, particularly for the films made earlier in the decade.

The Towering Inferno is perhaps Allen's grandest achievement; it took two of Hollywood's biggest production companies, Warner Bros. and Twentieth Century Fox, to get it made, and its budget of an estimated $14,000,000 was nearly three times more than that of *The Poseidon Adventure*. Although Gene Hackman, in the latter film, was riding high after his Academy Award-winning performance in *The French Connection* (1971) and there were other well-known faces in that film's cast, *The Towering Inferno* burns with an almost unbelievably powerful star wattage.

The all-star cast was not a new notion; it had enriched and blighted films in equal measure in the years before the disaster films of the 1970s. Biblical epics, such as *The Greatest Story Ever Told* (1965) were often laden with the stars of the day, whilst war films have often carried the weight of an all-star cast: *The Longest Day* (1962, featuring John Wayne, Henry Fonda and Robert Mitchum), *The Great Escape* (1963, featuring Steve McQueen, Richard Attenborough and James

Garner) and, possibly the starriest of all, *A Bridge Too Far* (1977, featuring Michael Caine, Sean Connery, Gene Hackman, Laurence Olivier...) are just three of many examples from this particular genre.

More recent examples include *Ocean's 11* (2001) and its sequels and *Bobby* (2006). All seem to be trying to make a statement with their big, starry casts: look at us, they appear to be saying – we must be good because we have so many big names! Some films sink under the weight of their casts, with the sight of an endless parade of stars obscuring the film's narrative. Some succeed, not least because audiences have fun spotting their favourite stars and are seduced by the spectacle of familiar faces, and, the film-makers hope, by the sense of gravity and glamour that an all-star cast can bring to a movie.

Theme

Corruption versus integrity

There are clear examples of corruption at the beginning of the film as James Duncan (William Holden) discovers that his son-in-law, Roger Simmons (Richard Chamberlain), has ignored safety regulations for the electrical wiring used throughout the building. Although Duncan does not know about this it is clear from the film that he is guilty of trying to keep building costs to a minimum. The notion of corruption is a key theme in 1970's cinema; either for financial or political gain, corruption was seen by the public as a very real and dangerous threat to democracy and personal freedom.

In the United States people had become disillusioned with their government's handling of the Vietnam War, which would end in humiliation for the American army, and the Watergate scandal of 1972, in which President Nixon was implicated in corrupt practices, eventually leading to his resignation in 1974. Around the world oil shortages and economic recession resulted in rather dismal conditions after many years of economic growth and increasing opportunity. Britain was particularly hit by the recession, which brought about rising unemployment, fuel rationing and strikes. In this climate, film-makers portrayed the corruption in many guises as the few got richer and more powerful, often at the expense of the many.

The Towering Inferno touches on this atmosphere of corruption, prompted by greed, and indeed, seems to take some pleasure in putting its wealthy and privileged characters in a precarious position, threatening them with ever more dangerous situations. Duncan's arrogance and belief that they are untouchable at the top of the building also underlines the negative representation of the elite.

The building itself is a symbol of man's folly, of greed and hubris. The fire fighters (see Representation section) and, to some extent, the architect (Paul Newman) are representative of integrity, a counterpoint to the avarice and blinkered vision of those who have created this particular disaster. At the film's denouement the final exchange between the chief and the architect focuses on the need for a change of direction, for integrity to overcome corruption and narrow-mindedness:

> Doug Roberts, the architect (to Susan Franklin): I don't know. Maybe they just oughta leave it [the burnt-out skyscraper] the way it is. Kinda shrine to all the bullshit in the world.
>
> *Chief O'Hallorhan enters*
>
> O'Hallorhan: You know, we were lucky tonight. Body count's less than two hundred. You know, one of these

days you're gonna kill 10,000 in one of these fire traps. And I'm gonna keep eating smoke and bringing out bodies... until someone asks us how to build 'em.

Roberts: Okay, I'm asking.

O'Hallorhan: You know where to reach me. So long, architect.

Chief O'Hallorhan joins a long line of Seventies characters fighting against 'bullshit', just as most of Steve McQueen's characters had done in his previous roles. He breathes the same anti-heroic air as the crusading journalists in *All the President's Men* (1976) fighting government corruption in the Watergate scandal; the eponymous hero of *Serpico* (1973) fighting police corruption and Joe Frady coming up against the unseen and deadly power of the establishment in *The Parallax View* (1974).

SELECT FILMOGRAPHY OF MAIN PRODUCERS AND CAST

John Guillerman, 1925, Director

I Was Monty's Double, 1958
Tarzan's Greatest Adventure, 1959
The Blue Max, 1966
The Bridge at Remagen, 1969
The Towering Inferno, 1974
King Kong, 1976
Death on the Nile, 1978

Irwin Allen, 1916-91, Producer/Director

The Lost World, 1960
Voyage to the Bottom of the Sea, 1961

The Poseidon Adventure, 1972
The Towering Inferno, 1974
The Swarm, 1978
Beyond the Poseidon Adventure, 1979
When Time Ran Out..., 1980

Steve McQueen, 1930–1980, Actor

The Magnificent Seven, 1960
The Great Escape, 1963
The Cincinnati Kid, 1965
The Thomas Crown Affair, 1968
Bullitt, 1968
The Getaway, 1972
Papillion, 1973
The Towering Inferno, 1974

Paul Newman, 1925-2008, Actor

The Hustler, 1961
Hud, 1963
Cool Hand Luke, 1967
Butch Cassidy and the Sundance Kid, 1969
The Sting, 1973
The Towering Inferno, 1974
When Time Ran Out..., 1980
The Verdict, 1982
The Color of Money, 1986
The Hudsucker Proxy, 1990
Road to Perdition, 2002

REPRESENTATION

Fire fighters

As the opening titles come to a close the following text appears: 'To those who give their lives so that others might live – To the fire fighters of the world – This picture is gratefully dedicated.' This type of dedication is reminiscent of the sort that appeared at the beginning of films during World War Two, praising those who had fought for their countries. This link and the prominence of the dedication signal that the film will portray the fire fighters in a very positive light, praising their virtues and presenting them as heroes. Throughout the film they are shown to be selfless heroes who think nothing of their own safety when trying to save others.

The first shots of the fire fighters, as they race to the scene of the fire, show them in spectacular and impressive fashion; their gleaming fire engines and cars race through the streets, the loud diegetic sound of their sirens adding to the sense of their importance and the danger into which they are plunging.

The film is full of incidents where the fire fighters are shown to be heroic, but also to be just ordinary people doing extraordinary things. Fire chief O'Hallorhan is played by Steve McQueen (see Actors, below), a major star at the time and regarded as an action hero and the epitome of 'cool', which inflects the fire fighters with an extra element of glamour and appeal to the audience.

Actors

Steve McQueen

In the decades since Steve McQueen's death he has become an icon, the essence of 'cool' and lauded by books, magazines

and documentaries. This public persona was forged, initially, in the television series *Wanted Dead or Alive*, where he played a charismatic bounty hunter. He moved on to the big screen, upstaging stars Frank Sinatra in *Never So Few* (1958) and Yul Brynner in *The Magnificent Seven* (1960). The 1960s confirmed his style as a man of action with *The Great Escape* (1963), *Hell is for Heroes* (1963), *The Cincinnati Kid* (1966), and *Bullitt* (1968). Beyond his unconventional good looks and bad boy image there was his passion for motorcars and motorbikes, and his considerable talent at a high level of competition.

The 1970s saw him continue to secure his position as one of Hollywood's biggest stars with roles in *The Getaway* (1971), *Junior Bonner* (1972), *Papillon* (1973) and *The Towering Inferno* (1974). Despite being one of the most popular and highest paid actors of his generation he continued to be plagued by insecurities, particularly in regards to his status as a film star. He needed to measure himself against his contemporaries and there was no bigger rival at this time than Paul Newman.

McQueen had watched Newman's success with interest ever since he landed a small role in Newman's breakthrough film in 1956, *Somebody Up There Likes Me*. McQueen had later turned down a chance to star alongside Newman in *Butch Cassidy and the Sundance Kid* (1969), which went on to be a massive hit, but *The Towering Inferno* proved to be an opportunity for McQueen to flex his film star muscles. This was epitomised in discussions over which actor would be billed first in the opening titles. The final decision satisfied both with McQueen getting the all-important left-hand side credit, albeit slightly lower than Newman's name to the right.

McQueen only made three more films before his death in 1980; he was a wealthy man and seemed satisfied that he had reached the pinnacle of his career. His next film after the Hollywood gloss of *The Towering Inferno* was the Ibsen adaptation, *An Enemy of the People* (1978), where he was almost unrecognisable with untidy hair and beard, a complete rejection of his superstar persona, and with not an action scene in sight.

McQueen's legacy can be seen in many of the action stars that followed: Bruce Willis, Russell Crowe and Matt Damon amongst others. But more than this, his reform school youth and premature death at the age of 50 have given him something of the James Dean aura: unconventional and rebellious, an icon with a mesmerising screen presence and a commitment to action rather than words.

Paul Newman

Paul Newman made his name in Robert Wise's *Somebody Up There Likes Me* and a string of roles where he portrayed anti-heroes. He was compared to James Dean and Marlon Brando, and went on to carve out a very successful and long career as a versatile actor, attempting both action and more intellectually challenging roles.

After Robert Wise's film he appeared as Billy the Kid in *The Left-Handed Gun* (1958), 'Fast' Eddie in *The Hustler* (1961), and as the eponymous anti-hero in *Hud* (1963) and *Cool Hand Luke*

(1967). In *Butch Cassidy and the Sundance Kid* and *The Sting* (1973), two of his most successful films, he starred alongside another superstar of the late 1960s and 1970s, Robert Redford.

Newman continued to make films throughout the next three decades, although his choices were more personal and played less to his superstar status and more to his interest in challenging roles. Whilst these were not always well-received by audiences, they are a fascinating insight into his interests and self-awareness of his superstar status. Both John Huston's *The Life and Times of Judge Roy Bean* (1972) and Robert Altman's *Buffalo Bill and the Indians* (1976) are 'revisionist' Westerns where the hero status of Western stereotypes are debunked and their actions are demythologised, as if Newman was unwrapping his own superstar persona.

Newman continued to make films until 2007 when he officially retired. In the last 30 years of his career he made a number of liberal-minded films such as *Absence of Malice* (1981) and *The Verdict* (1982), playing often compromised or flawed characters who seek redemption by fighting against powerful or corrupt institutions.

Like McQueen, Paul Newman was a very private man who eschewed the superstar lifestyle, increasingly playing against type in his later films. Both McQueen and Newman would play ageing lawmen in *The Hunter* (1980) and *Fort Apache, the Bronx* (1981) respectively, undermining their action hero personas with comic representations of men who are a little too old to be doing their jobs, but who maintain their dignity in an ever-changing world.

One other connection between the two actors was their love of fast cars. They both raced competitively and took risks that would be almost unthinkable for modern-day actors and in the prevailing health and safety conscious climate.

Newman's last screen appearance was in *Road to Perdition* (although he voiced one of the characters in the animated *Cars* (2006)), his longevity perhaps diminishing his cult status compared to McQueen, who died relatively young. However, he is one of the few lead actors to have forged a career over so many decades, witnessing countless changes in the film industry. His death in September 2008 brought an outpouring of goodwill and admiration for his film work, as well as his personal graciousness and charitable deeds.

TEXTUAL ANALYSIS

The observation elevator (DVD Chapter 31, 1:51:25)

Summary

The scene opens by reinforcing the links between some of the characters that will figure predominantly during the action that follows. Doug Roberts (Paul Newman) and Susan (Faye Dunaway) kiss, as do Harlee Claiborne (Fred Astaire) and Lisolette (Jennifer Jones); there is also a fond farewell between Mayor Ramsey (Jack Collins) and his wife (Sheila Mathews). This helps to emphasise their strong bonds and adds to the emotional impact on the audience as the next action set piece takes shape. A group of women and children leave in the observation elevator which is then disabled by an explosion as it descends, causing Lisolette to fall to her death. Chief O'Hallorhan (Steve McQueen) is lowered onto its roof by a helicopter to attach a winch, and the elevator is successfully lowered to the ground.

Camerawork

There are a series of close-ups of the main couples as the women gaze at their husbands and lovers. The doors close on them and the audience is drawn into this human drama as a result; these are not just faceless characters but people with personalities and relationships to which the audience can relate. The lift doors slide shut casting a shadow over Susan's face and then obscuring it completely, suggesting the danger that she will face. To further emphasise her and her companions' peril, the next shot shows them shrouded in darkness; the camera looks down onto the group, a high angle shot, which helps underline their vulnerability.

The elevator moves out of shot, the downward motion suggesting that they are descending into danger and that they are now at the mercy of the fire. The low angle long shot of the tiny elevator perched on the edge of the inferno reinforces the helplessness of the occupants, the flames lying in wait, and the use of pyrotechnics (the explosions) to further increase the sense of danger.

After a cut back to those left in the Promenade Room, the next shot shows a high angle long shot of the elevator, emphasising its precariousness. There follows a number of shots to show the struggle to fix a line between the burning building and an adjacent one in order to effect a rescue. The low angle shot of the helicopter, after the men have secured the line in the Promenade Room, helps to show its importance to the rescue, symbolising the only hope for those stranded. Another low angle shot, this time of the outside elevator, does not empower the occupants, as the framing captures the threat below, and then the explosion.

The framing becomes increasingly tight in the next three shots, focusing on the elevator and the occupants and increasing the intensity of the action with the different angles ensuring that the explosion is even more spectacular. The close-up from within the elevator adds to the confusion of the moment, and Lisolette's fall is seen from three angles to heighten the sense of drama and horror; the low angle long shot of the falling body is particularly effective.

The zoom in to the elevator and its screaming occupants helps to intensify the terror, whilst the cut-away shots of the fire chief relieve the tension for a few moments. The following low angle long shot of the elevator returns the audience to the focus of the scene, and the framing again underlines its vulnerability, the viewpoint putting the audience in a similar position as that of a helpless bystander looking up from

street level. The medium shot of the stranded group returns the audience to the very human drama unfolding inside the elevator.

The few minutes that then elapse, as the fire fighters and other personnel set up the breeches' buoy, which then takes one woman across from the burning building to safety, heightens the audience's anxiety to see the outcome of the elevator scene. As the fire chief is winched up by the helicopter to begin the rescue, the shot is again at a low angle. It frames the fiery edifice with the relatively small helicopter, highlighting the danger of this rescue attempt. The shot that returns us to the elevator is a medium one, reminding the audience of the occupant's plight. There is also a long shot of the fire chief suspended from the helicopter, emphasising his exposure to peril. The subsequent combination of shots from outside and within the elevator are underscored by using POV shots of the fire fighters as they look down at the big drop below, connecting the audience with the enormity of their task.

There is one final sequence from the Promenade Room which serves to heighten our anticipation of what is happening below in the elevator; the shot of Patty on the breeches' buoy is taken from above, with the massive drop and burning building beneath her. The final section of the rescue is comprised of mostly medium shots, charting the rescue attempt, each showing the fire fighters on the elevator's roof from a different

perspective to maintain audience interest. Shots looking up to the helicopter and then down to the ground from the elevator roof maintain the tension of the sequence as the elevator edges towards the ground and safety.

Sound

As the occupants of the elevator exchange last glances with their loved ones the non-diegetic music swells, a strings-led orchestral piece which is romantic sounding, but which turns sombre and discordant as the doors close, symbolising the pain felt by those left behind and the danger into which those in the elevator are descending. The diegetic sound is dominated by the helicopter, emphasising its importance to the rescue attempts in this scene, but also adding to the chaos of the scene with its deafening noise. Additionally, the shouts and cries of those in the Promenade Room and the noise of the roaring wind outside create a cacophony of sound to heighten the tension.

When the rope is fired from the adjacent building the crash into the bar and the sound of breaking glass, coupled with people's screams, raises the level still further. The explosion is given greater power by being amplified, an eruption of noise, which is coupled with the occupants' screams. With the shot of the elevator's occupants in the immediate aftermath of the explosion the sound of the flames is emphasised, maintaining the level of threat to those in the elevator, and the whimpering cries for help add to their vulnerability.

As those in the Promenade Room continue to pull people to safety the wind continues to roar, emphasising the people's defencelessness in the face of elemental power. In the elevator rescue there is a disorientating wall of diegetic sound, primarily the helicopter, but also the flames, and then screams as another explosion erupts. There is one final burst of screams from the women and from the falling fire fighter to underline the final jarring shock (tragedy averted as he falls onto a massive rescue air bed). The final comforting sound of the metal of the elevator's base touching down onto the concrete and the low sound of sirens, and final rescue, underlines that they are all safe. It is important to note that, apart from the music at the start of the sequence, all sound is diegetic, imbuing a sense of gritty realism and authenticity to this daring rescue.

Editing

The juxtaposition of faces at the beginning of the sequence by cutting between the couples to be parted sets up the loving connections between them, helping the audience to empathise with their individual stories. The action then switches to a helicopter firing a rope and pulley to set up a breeches' buoy between the skyscraper and another. This interweaving of plot threads, or multi-stranding, occurs throughout the film through the use of cross-cutting which helps build up the tension by frustrating the audience's desire to see each plot strand completed, and heightening their anticipation.

The whole sequence is propelled by standard continuity editing which ensures that the narrative progresses without confusion and that there is a 'cause and effect' flow which is easy to follow for the audience. The pace of the editing is fairly slow throughout the sequence, the shots tending to linger on the dramatic scenes of rescue. The exceptions to this are when the initial explosion dislodges the elevator and the cutting pace increases to heighten the excitement, and when the second explosion causes the young fire fighter to fall. Here the cuts between him and the chief, who is holding onto him, are very rapid which again adds to the drama of the moment. Their two faces intercut to highlight that the fire fighter's fate rests with one man, the chief.

Mise-en-scène

The mise-en-scène is dominated by the building itself; shots of it and the raging fire are key to the power of the scene; its immense size gives the sequence a sense of awe for the audience. The Promenade Room is also an important part of the mise-en-scène; by this point in the film its grandeur has faded as dramatic events have unfolded. Now we see a battered room, windows broken and high winds blasting the interior. The elaborate bar, marble floor, decorative urns, flowers and ornate balustrades are now subject to the unstoppable forces of nature. Their deterioration is a reminder of how it looked at the beginning of the film and the damage that has been done, to be completed when the water tanks are destroyed in the film's finale. As such, just like the building itself, the Promenade Room is seen as a metaphor for man's folly brought about by hubris, the act of over-reaching and ignoring the obvious dangers, a narrative motif that runs through many disaster films.

Another aspect of the mise-en-scène that has deteriorated is the state of the guests. Their expensive dinner suits and gowns and immaculate hairstyles have degenerated to the point where they all appear dishevelled and any complacency, pomposity and elegance has disappeared. Indeed, for the audience, it is rather fascinating to witness the fate of this group of elite guests. Their mannerisms and gestures have moved from sophistication and calmness to disarray and panic, helping to underpin the terror of the scene.

The tower, the elevator and the helicopter are key components of the mise-en-scène. The tower is either a model or there are sections shown which are built sets, and its glass/steel structure emphasises that this is a modern and cutting-edge structure (for 1974 at least). It also carries resonance for a modern audience in the wake of the destruction of the World Trade Center in New York, the huge smoking edifice pre-echoing images of the destruction of the Twin Towers as the fire laps against the sides of the building and adds to the sense of threat. In the elevator itself, the women are all dressed in light, colourful gowns, emphasising their vulnerability amidst the destruction, their terrified expressions helping to underpin the tension.

On the ground floor the fire fighters are in uniform, but they are dishevelled and dirty, as are their faces, underlining the unpleasant and dangerous conditions in which they are working. The stretcher, the men sitting on the floor and their general exhausted demeanour is reminiscent of the aftermath of a battle.

The helicopter appears many times in the sequence as a symbol of hope and power - the 'RESCUE' signage serves as a constant reminder of its importance to the trapped guests. In contrast with the helicopter, the breeches' buoy is very fragile-looking and precarious, adding to the sense of danger as people are ferried from the burning building to safety.

The final section focuses on the elevator rescue. It looks flimsy and vulnerable; panes of glass are the only thing between its occupants and death and it is hanging from its partially severed cable next to the raging fire. It all paints a picture of extreme danger. To counter this there is the presence of the helicopter with its strong winch, and more importantly, the fire chief. His physical presence brings hope and a sense of control amidst the chaos. He is carried by the winch, demonstrating that he is a man of action equipped with the necessary hardware to effect a rescue. The audience has already seen him in a number of difficult positions and he has been seen to be brave and professional (the fact that the actor is Steve McQueen, star of many films where his heroics have saved the day, also injects a sense of security into this scene).

Colour and lighting

The colours are very muted throughout this sequence; everything is in darkness and only the female guests' dresses have any colour, but even these are subdued as their wearers have undergone all sorts of physical hardship and they have lost their sparkle. The men and fire fighters are generally in dark colours to add to the sombre palette of the sequence; the only vibrant colour is that of the fire which, of course, is the most dominant and powerful force on screen.

As it is night time the lighting is low-key, the characters struggling in the shadows of the Promenade Room or in and around the elevator. This adds authenticity because the lights have failed and helps emphasise the sense of chaos and panic amongst the trapped guests. The lighting in the elevator casts shadows over the faces of those inside, particularly Susan's; her eyes are in shadow, making her sense of fear all the more dramatic. When the explosion dislodges the elevator the light of the fires illuminates its occupants and their terrified facial expressions.

The area on ground level where the fire fighters are based is also shadowy, underpinning the downbeat atmosphere; they are exhausted and battered from their work. The rest of the sequence is played out in the shadows cast by the flames. The menace of the darkness adds a sense of drama to the events and the roaring flames cast an orange glow of intensity on the fire chief's face as he strains to hold onto the young fire fighter as the elevator is lowered. The flashing red lights of the rescue service vehicles below are beacons of safety contrasted with the turmoil of the darkness and the flames above.

'This is the disaster film which set the style for the genre in the decade to come.' Martyn Auty, *Time Out 14th Ed.*, **Time Out Guides Ltd., London, 2006.**

'*The Towering Inferno* is a brawny blockbuster of a movie, by far the best of the mid-1970s wave of disaster films. It's three hours long, it cost something like $13 million to make... and it's an example of Hollywood commercial moviemaking at its finest...

The Towering Inferno is, in fact, a masterpiece of stunt co-ordination and special effects. And there's never that phony feeling we got in *Earthquake*, when you could see where the high-rise set stopped and the painted flats began...[an] interesting question might involve the meaning of all those disaster films... Was it that during hard times and uncertain world conditions we turned to escapist entertainment? Perhaps when we fear for ourselves, we go to disaster movies to face and exorcise greater fears. Or perhaps Hollywood simply rediscovered a dependable old genre and reinvigorated it with millions of bucks and lots of big-name stars. It was the same approach that would work in later years with horror, science fiction and other durable genres: Throw stars and money at them, and they deliver. **Roger Ebert, 1974**

Chapter 4: Case Study 3 – *The Day After Tomorrow*

KEY FACTS

Release Date: 2004

Country of Origin: USA

Running Time: 124 minutes

Budget

$125,000,000

PRODUCTION NOTES

Production Companies

20th Century Fox

Centropolis Entertainment

Lions Gate Films

Mark Gordon Productions

Distributor

20th Century Fox

Marketing – The Title

The enigmatic title of the film suggests an inevitability about the events depicted, that eventually catastrophe will come to the world. It is designed to be unnerving and slightly oblique in order to pique the audience's curiosity.

Taglines

Where will you be?

> This was the main tagline that appeared on posters in the run-up to the film's release. It has a dual function; firstly, it helps generate interest in the film as an event, something not to be missed. Also, it suggests danger, an intimation that the events of the film could be about to happen, a device designed to draw in its prospective audience, holding the same resonance as other major events. People always talk about remembering where they were when US president, John F. Kennedy, was assassinated or when they heard about the attack on the World Trade Center in New York; this tagline echoes that sense of a memorable and devastating event.

Now it's fiction... Tomorrow it's real.

Nature has spoken.

10,000 years ago, one storm changed the face of our planet. On May 28, it will happen again.

> These three taglines are full of Hollywood excess, doom-laden and prophetic of catastrophe. Although somewhat tongue-in-cheek, they are designed to create an atmosphere, which suggests that the film's story and impact will be profound and earth-shattering. It is, of course, an attempt to link the possible threats of climate change with the experience of watching the film, thus, tapping into the current anxiety regarding climate change.

Whoever said "Tomorrow is another day"... didn't check the weather.

This year, a sweater won't do.

These two taglines have a more light-hearted message, which will be amusing for audiences, although they are still linked to the apocalyptic vision inherent in the other taglines.

Ultimately, all the taglines help connect the film with an important world issue, presenting a vision of the future which people can watch, be awestruck and unnerved by, but finally enjoy. In this way it becomes a 'must-see' film, wrapping up our genuine anxieties in an attractive Hollywood package, and allowing us to face our fears in a safe environment.

Posters

The dominant image in the poster above is that of the Statue of Liberty, an iconic symbol around the world, connoting freedom, justice and democracy. As with the poster campaign for *Cloverfield* (2007) the destruction of the monument is a key element and a very powerful image. In *Cloverfield* the statue is decapitated, a rather shocking image that suggests violent death, literally and metaphorically; indeed, that film does not end happily. In this *The Day After Tomorrow* image, the statue is threatened by ice but part of the head and outstretched arm

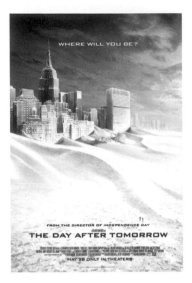

remain, a sign that hope may prevail, or that all is not lost, an idea in keeping with the message of the film.

This and other posters for the film have the same dominant colours, a combination of steely blue and black, signifying a colourless world devoid of vibrant life. Although the second poster (left) does not have an image of the Statue of Liberty, it is linked by the skyline of Manhattan, another iconic image of the United States and a symbol of vitality, progress and wealth for those who view Western images from a positive perspective.

New York, for many around the world, is the first city of the United States even though Washington D.C. is the capital, and an attack here is the most pertinent for audiences, particularly since 9/11. In both the posters this imposing skyline is made to look insignificant and vulnerable in the face of the colossal waves and the ice; the forces of nature are shown to be more than a match to any man-made structures. Apart from the tagline, 'Where will you be?', the other information is made up of the film's title and the line 'From The Director Of *Independence Day*', the latter helping to stimulate interest in audiences who like spectacular disaster blockbusters.

Film Trailer (US advance trailer)

The trailer intercuts real footage of natural disasters and people in danger with images from the film which are all scenes of devastation and action. This blurring of reality and fiction helps to add authenticity to the film, tapping into people's real fears about climate change and natural disasters. The opening 20th Century Fox ident has some subtle snowfall around it and changes in quality from pristine to something similar to CCTV footage or a domestic video, as if there has been some great disturbance. The text which appears across the screen prophesises the disaster to come, linking the events of the film with cataclysmic events from the past. The text is bold and impressive, almost biblical in its authoritative appearance; as well as being a steely white/blue, again linking to the idea of an ice age; it moves towards the foreground of the screen, which adds to the sense of threat ('it's coming!'). The swirling clouds, lightning and dark colours suggest some sort of apocalypse, which connects to the events of the film. The music begins with a haunting choral piece and again echoes the biblical/religious tone of the events depicted in the film.

Synopsis

The film charts the onset of a new ice age triggered by global warming. Climatologist Jack Hall predicts the catastrophe. There are numerous worldwide incidents of extreme weather building up to a number of superstorms. These initiate the spread of the new ice age and we see the cities of Los Angeles and New York being destroyed by tornadoes and tidal waves respectively. A climate research station in Scotland also monitors the catastrophic conditions, but the scientists eventually succumb to the effects of the storm. Amidst the destruction and loss of life one group of people, including Jack Hall's son, Sam, manage to survive at the New York Public Library. Jack and two colleagues make the journey to New York to find Sam with a few survivors. The storms eventually pass, but the view from space reveals that the northern hemisphere is now covered with ice.

Commentary

German-born Roland Emmerich has made a career in Hollywood with disaster films. His is the 'cinema of the apocalypse'. He has made a series of films that portray the world plunging into nightmarish catastrophes. In *Independence Day* (1996) the earth is under threat from aliens, whilst *Godzilla* (1998) sees yet another monster destroying their favourite playground, New York. *The Day After Tomorrow* will be followed by *2012* (2009), another foray into apocalyptic futures. Emmerich and Hollywood, of course, know an entertaining and lucrative concept when they see it; indeed, Emmerich has dedicated himself to this genre. But it seems that it is not entirely about money for he is keenly interested in taking the warnings about the planet to as wide an audience as possible. Making a series of blockbuster disaster productions, all high-concept films, he has been able to satisfy studio executives, audiences and his personal agenda.

Theme

Global warming

The film's main narrative thrust details the catastrophic effects of global warming. With the disintegration of the polar ice caps the temperature of the North Atlantic Current plummets, which sets in motion a chain of events that lead to the creation of superstorms that bring a new ice age to the northern hemisphere. The threat and reality of global warming have been in the public conscience and on the political agenda for many years, and it seems that we may now be seeing the very real effects of carbon emissions on the natural environment.

Although the speed with which the adverse conditions take effect in the film have been disputed by scientists, there is still much which chimes with current fears: rising water levels, increased flooding, more severe storms and unusual weather patterns. The accelerated weather changes are perhaps unrealistic and suit Hollywood demands for immediate spectacular action, but the film-makers' avowed intent is to shock and to warn. In this way the film taps into our deepest fears about the planet's future, albeit with a Hollywood gloss.

SELECT FILMOGRAPHY OF MAIN PRODUCERS AND CAST

Roland Emmerich, 1955, Director, Writer, Producer

Universal Soldier, 1992
Independence Day, 1996
Godzilla, 1998
The Patriot, 2000
The Day After Tomorrow, 2004
10,000 BC, 2008
2012, 2009

Denis Quaid, 1954, Actor

Breaking Away, 1979
The Long Riders, 1980

All Night Long, 1981
The Night the Lights Went Out in Georgia, 1981
Stripes, 1981
Jaws 3-D, 1983
The Right Stuff, 1983
Dreamscape, 1984
Enemy Mine, 1985
The Big Easy, 1987
Innerspace, 1987
Suspect, 1987
D.O.A., 1988
Great Balls of Fire!, 1989
Postcards from the Edge, 1990
Wyatt Earp, 1994
Dragonheart, 1996
The Parent Trap, 1998
Any Given Sunday, 1999
Traffic, 2000
The Rookie, 2002
Cold Creek Manor, 2003
The Alamo, 2004
The Day After Tomorrow, 2004
Flight of the Phoenix, 2004
Yours, Mine and Ours, 2005
American Dreamz, 2006
Vantage Point, 2008
Smart People, 2008

Jake Gyllenhaal, 1980, Actor

October Sky, 1999
Donnie Darko, 2001
Bubble Boy, 2001

Lovely & Amazing, 2001
Highway, 2002
Moonlight Mile, 2002
The Good Girl, 2002
The Day After Tomorrow, 2004
Brokeback Mountain, 2005
Jarhead, 2005
Proof, 2005
Zodiac, 2007
Rendition, 2007
Brothers, 2008

REPRESENTATION

Politicians

Hollywood has not often portrayed politicians in a favourable light. The exposé of President Nixon's criminal activities whilst in office was the subject of Alan J. Pakula's *All The President's Men* (1976); an earlier film, Michael Ritchie's *The Candidate* (1972) explores the compromising nature of political power whilst Barry Levinson's *Wag The Dog* (1997) satirises the power of spin doctors to manipulate public perception of their political leaders. In *The Day After Tomorrow* the US president is shown to be rather impotent in the face of the oncoming catastrophe, vacillating between plans and relying on others to make the decisions. The vice-president is portrayed as a ruthless and aggressive politician who initially stands against the climatologist's proposals.

The salvation of the planet does not lie in the hands of the politicians but with the scientists, personified by Dennis Quaid's character, who predict, act and suggest survival scenarios. Indeed, director Emmerich seems fond of showing the ineffectiveness of political institutions; the most memorable image from his previous end-of-the-world film, *Independence Day* (1996), being the spectacular destruction of the iconic White House, a symbol of political impotence in the film as the President initially tries to appease the aliens.

Los Angeles

Although the destruction of New York is the centre piece of the film, the scene showing the tornadoes ripping apart Los Angeles is an interesting representation of this famous city. The Californian city, home to Hollywood, has been the backdrop to many films. It has been an important presence in brooding thrillers about the underbelly of the dream factory with such films as *Sunset Boulevard* (1950) and, more recently, *The Player* (1992) and *Mulholland Drive* (2001). It has also been shown as fairly barbaric in films like *Assault On Precinct 13* (1976) or the futuristic *Escape From LA* (1996), both directed by John Carpenter.

In *The Day After Tomorrow* Los Angeles is little more than a plaything for the incredible power of the tornadoes. As the Hollywood sign and the Capitol Records building are pulverised it is both a signal that Mother Nature is no respecter of iconic man-made constructions and a playful joke at the expense of the entertainment capital of the world. Even Hollywood, with all its power and creativity to conjure up such images, would be no match for the real thing.

Actors

Dennis Quaid

Quaid's career has had a number of high points, but there have also been many poorly-received films, among them the soggy sequel, *Jaws 3D* (1983). The successful *Breaking Away* (1979) was followed by the interesting revisionist Western, *The Long Riders* (1980), where he appeared with his brother Randy. Although a leading man he is certainly not an actor who has the same level of stardom and audience pulling power as contemporaries like Mel Gibson or Tom Hanks. Notable films are *The Right Stuff* (1983), *The Big Easy* (1987), *Postcards From The Edge* (1990) and particularly *Far From Heaven* (2002), his most critically acclaimed performance where he played against type as a middle-class husband in 1950s America who finds himself drawn into a homosexual affair. After many stereotypically macho characterisations over the years it is ironic that this proved to be his most rewarding to date.

Jake Gyllenhaal

Gyllenhaal is part of a film-making family; his father is a director whilst his mother is a screenwriter and sister Maggie is a successful actress (*Secretary*, 2002; *The Dark Knight*, 2008). Gyllenhall's performances have concentrated on vulnerable and troubled characterisations, typified by his titular role in *Donnie Darko* (2001). However, his career failed to ignite after appearing in this cult classic and he followed

with a number of films that were not critical or financial successes. But in the wake of *The Day After Tomorrow* he put together a string of well-received films that showed his versatility. He next played a cowboy in *Brokeback Mountain* (2005) opposite Heath Ledger's Ennis del Mar, with whom he has a love affair. This was followed by three very different roles in the films *Jarhead* (2005), *Proof* (2005) and *Zodiac* (2007), all helping to cement this young actor's popularity with audiences, particularly amongst 20-somethings.

TEXTUAL ANALYSIS

Tornadoes hit LA (DVD Chapter 10, 0:26:00)

Summary

The city of Los Angeles in California is hit by a number of tornadoes, an event caused by the rapidly changing global climate conditions. It is unprecedented for the city and it unsurprisingly attracts the attention of the media, who try to record their destructive power. In the course of the sequence, vehicles are thrown by the tornadoes and we witness the destruction of numerous buildings as they gather force. Two meteorologists and a news reporter are introduced to the audience but then killed by the tornadoes.

Camerawork

The swooping aerial shot that begins the sequence gives the audience a helicopter's perspective; the shot is exhilarating and dynamic, adding to the spectacular revelation as the camera tilts upwards that Los Angeles is being devastated by four tornadoes. The next shot, a medium close-up of the television reporter in the helicopter, helps to focus on an individual with whom the audience can identify; the disaster scene to follow is much more effective when the audience can empathise with some of the individuals that will be involved. The camera then begins to crane from the ground upwards, inspiring a feeling of awe as we see a tornado ripping through a building, followed by another moving aerial shot of one tornado funnel which makes the action even more dynamic.

After a couple more shots of specific individuals, a meteorologist and the television reporter on the helicopter, which again cement the audience's identification, there is another moving shot, a tracking shot, which then cranes downwards so that we identify with another television reporter and his experiences. The audience, and the reporter, think any spectacle and possible danger will come from the tornado that his colleague is filming out of the side window but the next shot from within their van suddenly and violently presents a far greater threat as cars are thrown onto the road from another tornado in front of them. The camera is now within their van and we share their POV, adding to the audience's first-hand experience of the danger as a car hurtles towards us. The next shot takes us out of the van, and the flying car heads straight for the camera, totally immersing the audience in the action. The shot is repeated with a second car that slams into us and not the van, which swerves to avoid it.

We then return to another personal drama as one meteorologist in an office speaks to his colleague who has stopped on the streets. We see his POV as the camera tilts up to show a tornado tearing through another building. After a few shots of both men, with the man outside getting back into a car, we see his car being crushed by a bus from an aerial angle. The distance of the shot underlines the power of the storm and makes the vehicle look like a tiny plaything being thrown by the tornado.

As the car is flattened the shot switches to a close-up of the television screen that the other meteorologist is watching; the audience sees both the film-makers' shot of the death and the corresponding news report, giving it a sense of verisimilitude. Our sympathy with these characters is increased because we

can see the profound effect these events are having on the general public.

We now see the news reporter and his cameraman, who were originally in the van, on a television screen as they report from the streets, again adding a sense of reality to the events. The audience is then brought into his world with the next shot from behind the news cameraman's back, slowly tracking around the two men to frame not one but two tornadoes that surround them. The next few shots are from within the meteorologist's office, the shots framing his, a woman's and a cleaner's frightened reaction to the shaking building, which helps to focus the audience's connection with individual characters' reactions to the storm.

Outside, the camera tracks around the reporter and cameraman to reveal a threat that the reporter cannot see, a flying billboard, which slams into him. The next shot is a high angle aerial one which gives the audience a spectacular view of the power of the tornadoes; it looks like an apocalyptic vision of destruction and puts all the earlier and close-up scenes of individual turmoil into a wider context. Two medium close-ups of the office meteorologist and his lover ensure that the spectacle continues to have a human face and we only see their reactions to the oncoming destruction.

The next few medium close-ups of the cleaner in the same office continue the suspense as the audience is denied a view

of events outside the building. The camerawork maintains the tension as we slowly track behind the cleaner as he walks towards the door emitting an eerie bright light, and then with the close-up of the doorknob. The revelatory shot emphasises the spectacular destruction wrought by the tornado. The aerial shot tracks back from the cleaner as he appears in the doorway and sees the whole side of the building ripped off. The wide angle shot reveals the massive destruction and chaos that the tornadoes have caused, and the inevitable human loss of life.

Sound

There is a combination of both diegetic and non-diegetic sound throughout this sequence. The non-diegetic music is a powerful orchestral score with emphasis on the brass instruments that creates a brooding and threatening atmosphere. When cutting back to the characters watching events on television the levels lessen somewhat and then peak again when we see visuals of the tornadoes, emphasising their power and threat. There is also a repetitive drumming beat, like a military piece of music, which has tremendous force and mirrors the idea of the tornadoes as an unstoppable entity.

The diegetic sound ratchets up the tension of the scene. Voices of the reporters and their dramatic intonation and words help to increase the level of tension and an almost ever-present sound is that of the wind and the noise of debris flying. They contrast with the relative quiet of the office interiors and the places where people are watching events on television; this gives the storm shots extra aural power and continually unnerves the viewer.

As larger objects are thrown in the air we hear increased levels of noise, the sound of screeching and crunching metal as the cars hit the road, for example, adding to the impact of the visuals. The death of the meteorologist in his car is accentuated by the sound of the telephone line disconnecting as the bus crushes his car while his colleague is speaking to him. The chaotic sounds eventually reach inside the office as the tornado approaches, and the noise of objects rattling and smashing accentuates the sense of confusion and impending doom.

The reporter's death is underlined by a sickening thud as the hoarding slams into him and then the non-diegetic music begins to reach a thunderous and malevolent climax as we see the wide shot of the skyscrapers buffeted by the tornadoes. The sound of the helicopter is muted and seems puny compared with the music, which mirrors the storm's power. The music swells and then recedes as the screen goes black, the noise of screeching metal and rattling also dissipating.

There now begins a build-up to the final dramatic shot; the sounds are muted, punctuated by the odd exploding light as the cleaner walks up to open the door and reveals the devastation. As he nears the door the music becomes louder and is dominated by an eerie repetition of orchestral strings, whilst the diegetic sound is of a sinister howling wind, much less powerful than before but underlining the tension.

As we see that the building has been stripped of an exterior wall on one side the music swells and a haunting vocal dominates the soundtrack; it is a ghostly sound, appropriate for such a scene of death and devastation. The only diegetic sounds are the lightly blowing wind, a lonely sound which again highlights the sense of catastrophe and loss, as well as the forlorn noise of unanswered alarms, which often follows devastation in our modern cities in the wake of destruction, whether man-made or natural.

Editing

The editing in this sequence helps to propel the narrative along, cutting between a number of different story threads in order to retain audience interest in the unfolding narrative. The film shows a little of each character's story in fragments, cutting to a new story to maintain the levels of tension; we see the reporter in the plane, the reporter on the streets, the meteorologist in the office and his boss who is trying to drive to the office. The cuts from these individuals to shots of the tornadoes help to connect them to the ferocious storm and emphasises their vulnerability.

The editing has a fairly fast pace, underlining the frenetic nature of the action, especially when there is a moment of intense action, such as when the cars are being blown towards the television reporter's van. The cuts occur as the cars 'hit' the camera, drawing the audience into the action as if the flying cars are blotting us out. The rapid cutting between the meteorologist in the office and his boss outside helps develop the link between them and builds to the climax of the latter's death in the car, the horror of which is doubled with the cut to the television screen which allows the meteorologist to see his colleague's death 'live' on television.

The editing gathers momentum as the office workers and cleaner feel the full force of the tornado approaching the building, but then it slows again as the cleaner makes his way to the door that will reveal the devastation. The eventual cut from inside the building takes quite a long time compared to the rapid editing before, cleverly priming the audience's anticipation to see what has happened beyond the door.

Mise-en-scène

The snaking motorway, the helicopter and skyscrapers in the background confirm that this is indeed a modern city, but one which is defenceless against the elemental power of tornadoes. The CGI tornadoes dominate the whole sequence, ripping apart the man-made structures as if they were made of paper. They are swirling masses of debris, gigantic funnels of destruction that dwarf all the buildings. The destruction of the Hollywood sign, an iconic symbol of the American film industry and world-wide cultural power, like that of the Statue of Liberty in *Cloverfield*, highlights an attack on symbols that are important to the American people. (It is also an elaborate in-joke with a Hollywood film showing the destruction of the famous Hollywood landmark).

As will also be noted in the *Cloverfield* textual analysis, (case study 4) there is an emphasis on *recording* the event, reflecting the modern desire to capture all things on tape/digitally. Here, the helicopter news team and those on the ground are driven to record at all costs, regardless of their personal safety, and a bystander is also shown videoing the tornadoes rather than escaping. There are also shots of the television audience watching the events; it all reflects the media-saturated world where we are constantly fed images from around the globe.

In a blatant piece of product placement, it is also easy to identify the Fox News logo, part of Rupert Murdoch's News Corporation, which owns both Fox News and 20th Century Fox, the film's main financial backer and distributor. In this way the multi-media conglomerate manages to promote other parts of its business while simultaneously reinforcing the text's verisimilitude. The Capitol Records building is quite clearly seen in the path of a tornado and it is soon subject to its ferocious power. Although not as famous an image as the Hollywood sign it is still an iconic structure on the Los Angeles skyline and would certainly signal to Americans that anything iconic or sacred to the American people is vulnerable to the enormous power of nature.

The mise-en-scène is then dominated by the tornadoes and the effect of their force: aeroplanes are lifted and cars are thrown through the air, all demonstrating to the audience their deadly power. The shots continue to be filled by swirling debris, caught up in the tornadoes, a maelstrom of destruction, with one news reporter capturing the full horror of the scene from ground level, surrounded by flying paper with CGI tornadoes in the background. The meteorologist's office is full of high-tech machinery, all designed to monitor the weather, but now rather ineffectual in the face of the reality of what lies outside. The wildly erratic recorder of atmospheric activity is an unnerving indicator of the storm's ferocity, increasing the level of tension. The rooms and objects in the building are also rattling and rocking to help emphasise the strength of the tornadoes outside.

The mise-en-scène of the next shot is again dominated by swirling debris as the reporter continues to comment on events; the dominant image is the flying advertising hoarding as it flattens the man. The image of a scantily-clad woman on the hoarding does give the moment a slightly humorous edge, as does the way he is flattened so suddenly; there is a comic-book element to the violence at this point.

The CGI shot of the cityscape is full of swirling winds weaving amidst the skyscrapers, producing a particularly menacing image and vision of the tornadoes' power. The final segment is dominated by the human reaction to the tornadoes from within the meteorologist's office, the room continuing to shake and the occupants' faces full of fear. The final image of the devastated skyscrapers, a CGI scene, reveals again the tremendous destructive force of the tornadoes. The tiny image of the cleaner in the open doorway on the side of one ravaged building underlines humanity's vulnerability and impotence in the face of such raw power.

Colour and lighting

The opening wide shot of Los Angeles with the four tornadoes bearing down on its centre is dominated by a dark shroud of clouds, draining the city of any colour and adding to the threatening atmosphere. The patch of bright sky to the left of frame is a reminder of what the sky should be, but it is quickly diminishing as the dark tornadoes spread. As well as the darkness the dominant colour is a lifeless, steely blue, mirroring the menace that these tornadoes will bring to LA. On the street the colours are also muted, and whenever there is a shot of the skyline we see darkness and a splash of red symbolising danger. The meteorologist's office is also dark, what lighting there is throwing shadows onto the characters' faces. The only shots where the characters are shown in even light are when we see the audience watching the television; they are, at present, in a safe place.

In the office, the woman, and then the meteorologist, are seen in shadow with flashing lights adding to the sense of threat. The final moments before the tornado hits the meteorologist's office are full of more shadows and flashing lights, highlighting the characters' terror. Ultimately, the screen goes black, signifying a deadly outcome. The lighting in the office corridor as the cleaner walks to the door is very menacing. A shaft of light is emitted from the door that he is approaching and the rest of the corridor is full of a sinister darkness, creating tension for the audience. The shaft of light does not offer hope, but seems almost supernatural and ominous as if from a horror film. The final image of the devastated skyscraper is again full of darkness and shadow, with just an edge of light. It is a picture of devastation and despair.

'He had aliens zap the Big Apple in *Independence Day*, and a latter-day Godzilla stomp it to mush. Now mayhem meister Emmerich floods the place with a tidal wave, then freezes it over for an encore. Thus is banished any inkling that 9/11 might have affected Hollywood's appetite for childlike destruction. But there's also a serious agenda beyond the usual CGI fiesta, since these rising sea levels and glacial temperatures result from melting polar ice caps altering the ocean currents, an unavoidable by-product of global warming... Connoisseurs of disaster-movie tack will be relieved to know their favourite elements remain intact, from slumming performers (boffin Holm turns ashen upon the realisation he's facing a snowy demise with only half a bottle of single malt), to dumb macho heroics (scientist Quaid's too late to save the world, so he'll make do with rescuing son Gyllenhaal from iced-in Manhattan), and the regulation child leukaemia 'victim in peril'.' Author: Trevor Johnston *Time Out Film Guide*

'...Emmerich has to entertain us with all the things we expect from group jeopardy and disaster films... The first ingredient is spectacular destruction, which his battalion of special effects experts provide. There is a little problem in making such a film in the wake of 11 September 2001. As the camera pans over the Manhattan skyline, we are only too aware of the absence of the World Trade Center. With footage of the demolition of the Twin Towers indelibly printed on our minds, can we pleasurably anticipate something similarly awful happening to New York for fun?

The answer lies in the fact that no one wrote about 9/11 without evoking disaster movies. Reality and cinema have become one in our media-saturated world...

The second ingredient of the disaster movie is human interest. We need a small bunch of survivors to identify with, and here that role is assigned to the family of Professor Hall, whose workaholism has led to a separation from his wife and neglect of his teenage son (Jake Gyllenhaal). Naturally the crisis draws them together, and dad undertakes a perilous redemptive journey to rescue the lad...

A third ingredient is the moral dimension, the apportioning of blame, and this usually reflects the temper of the times. The 1936 movie *San Francisco* presented the immoral world of the city before the judgment of the 1906 earthquake and then its subsequent rebuilding... Often there are negligent or hubristic scientists on hand to blame, but in this film they are all good men.' Philip French, *The Observer*, May 30 2004

Chapter 5: Case Study 4 – *Cloverfield*

KEY FACTS

Release Date: 2007

Country of Origin: USA

Running Time: 81 minutes

Budget

$25,000,000

PRODUCTION NOTES

Production Companies

Paramount Pictures

Bad Robot

Distributor

Paramount Pictures

Marketing – The Title

The title is deliberately innocuous, conjuring up an image of a rural and idyllic place, very much the opposite to the content of the film. It is a very unusual title for a big budget monster/ disaster film which would tend to sound much more dramatic. However, this atypical title is yet another ploy to generate interest in a film that claims to be actual found footage of the event depicted.

Tagline

Some Thing Has Found Us (as found on the principal theatrical posters)

> The breaking up of the word 'something' helps to give extra emphasis to the word 'thing' and its connotations of otherness and negativity; the fact that it 'has found us' suggests that we have been hunted.

Posters

The image of a decapitated Statue of Liberty is made prominent by being placed in the foreground against a large expanse of sky – our attention is thereby directed towards the missing element. She is gouged, with debris still falling from her, as if violated by something monstrous. There is a flow of water towards Manhattan, which directs the eye to the scarred buildings with smoke billowing from them, the sense of movement suggesting an unstoppable force. It is a scene of devastation full of menace and prompts a number of questions as to the source of this destruction. The dark clouds complete a picture of brooding threat and the whole image has an apocalyptic air. The small text, a date, effectively creates a sense of anticipation for the audience who will want answers to the questions posed by this poster. As such, it achieves its purpose, which is to stimulate interest in the film (this American one-sheet poster is known as an advance).

Other versions of the teaser include single words at the top of the picture, such as 'Monstrous', 'Terrifying' and 'Furious', adding to the posters' sense of menace and creating more intrigue around the film.

The British advance poster, known as a quad, is a landscape version of the American one-sheet; its format is equivalent to a widescreen film and, as such, its devastation and atmosphere of foreboding is given an epic scale.

Film trailer teaser

The film's initial trailer did not even use the title in order to generate increased audience interest and speculation, thus tying in with the poster campaign. This was shown before theatrical showings of *Transformers* in the summer of 2007, containing just images and the release date, allying *Cloverfield* to a successful action/science fiction film which targeted a similar demographic of teenagers. The rapidly edited footage, taken from near the beginning of the film, conveys the sense of a home video recording, both the very ordinary and then the terrible scenes of destruction.

Internet

Cloverfield, a film very much of the YouTube generation with its young cast, monster narrative, use of cutting-edge CGI and the handheld digital camera footage, was heavily marketed on the internet. On this platform, its chief audience demographic (approximately 15-25 years old) would delight in the intriguing and puzzling methods of marketing. By linking the film so closely to the internet through its marketing, the film connects with its audience.

The website address for the film is www.1-18-08.com, the date of the film's release in the United States, which was the focus for the film's advance posters. Of course, the date itself, with its repeated numbers has a certain distinction, just as J. J. Abrams' film *Mission Impossible III* opened on 5-05-06 in the United States and *The Omen* (synonymous with the Biblical numbers 666) was released across the world on 6-06-06.

1-18-08.com displays a number of photographs, some containing disturbing images, which can be flipped over to reveal messages. The overriding effect is disturbing, a puzzle to be pieced together by an audience that loves to solve puzzles, particularly those found in computer games. This website, part of the film's viral marketing campaign, initiated a high level of speculation amongst its target audience eager to know more about the content. The film also carried with it the imprimatur of a J. J. Abrams production. Abrams has a young, media-savvy fan base already eager for more of his work and accustomed to his marketing methods, as used for his television series, *Lost* (2004-present).

Other viral marketing strategies included the creation of websites focusing on fictitious companies associated with the film. The main ones are www.tagruato.jp and www.slusho.jp, the former being the name of the company that Rob

Hawkins is going to work for in Japan. One of this company's subsidiaries is the drinks company, Slusho! Both websites contain full company profiles and contact details, acting as further entry points into the world of the film, creating a ready-made mythology.

Prior to release, the clues, or supposed clues, on these websites helped to increase awareness about the film and spread word-of-mouth interest in its content. The drink Slusho! had already been mentioned in Abrams' earlier television series *Alias*, and this kind of intertextuality helped fuel audience interest with the new film project. The character, Marlena Diamond, also has a MySpace page, another way in which the film-makers imbue the other worldly events of the film with a patina of realism.

Synopsis

The film's narrative is video footage from a digital camera recovered by the United States Department of Defense in New York and discovered in an area that they have labelled US-447, originally known as Central Park. In the first part, Rob Hawkins (Michael Stahl-David) videos a girl, Beth (Odette Yustman), with whom he has just spent the night. We learn that prior to becoming lovers they had been friends. The footage then cuts to the preparations for a leaving party for Rob as he gets ready to go to a new job in Japan. Initially, the cameraman is Rob's brother, Jason (Mike Vogel), but he gives the camera over to their mutual friend, Hud (T.J. Miller), who films most of the succeeding events.

As the party gets into full swing it becomes apparent that Beth has not continued to see Rob in the intervening period. When Beth arrives at the party with another man, Rob's anger and jealousy forces a confrontation and she hurriedly leaves the party. Hud records this argument and tells Jason about it, who also tells his own girlfriend, Lily (Jessica Lucas). Hud also tries, unsuccessfully, to flirt with a girl called Marlena (Lizzy Caplan), who he has been attracted to for a long time.

A blackout and an earthquake-like shuddering of the building initiates the next segment of the footage as explosions and falling debris, including the head of the Statue of Liberty, indicate New York is under attack. It soon becomes clear that some sort of giant creature is destroying the city, causing a mass exodus from the area, Manhattan, where the monster is running amok. Rob, Jason, Lily and Marlena try to escape over the Brooklyn Bridge, but the monster destroys it and Jason is killed.

Rob receives a call from Beth to say that she is trapped in her apartment and the rest of the footage consists of the remaining four's attempt to rescue Beth alongside running battles between the military and the monster and fighting small, but deadly creatures that fall from the monster and attack humans. Although Lily eventually escapes, Marlena and Hud are killed, leaving Rob and Beth to record their final goodbyes as explosions destroy everything around them in Central Park. The footage then cuts back to Rob and Beth from a few weeks before, happy together and on a trip to the amusement park on Coney Island.

Commentary

J.J. Abrams has become an important force in Hollywood since the late-1990s. He has proved to be extremely versatile in his work, with writing, producing and directing credits to his name in both film and TV. Although one of his early television creations, *Felicity* (1998-2002), revolves around a university student, much of his work has a science fiction basis. Television series such as *Alias* (2001–2006) and *Lost* established him in the TV industry, but he has also forged a career in films, co-writing the script for *Armageddon* (1998), directing *Mission Impossible: III* (2006) and *Star Trek* (2009), as well as producing *Cloverfield*. With his production company, Bad Robot, he has also gone on to make a new television drama, *Fringe* (2008-9), and there are possible plans to make a sequel to *Cloverfield* and another film project, *The Invisible Woman*.

The success of *Cloverfield* and his television series, *Alias* and *Lost*, has given Abrams the power to flex his creative muscles in Hollywood, signing deals with both Paramount and Warner Bros for future projects. There are many parallels between Abrams and disaster film-maker, Irwin Allen, responsible for *The Towering Inferno* amongst many others. Like Allen before him, Abrams works in both television and film, producing dramas that focus on action, adventure and sometimes have a science fiction or fantasy angle.

Theme

9/11 and 'Western anxiety'

Cloverfield is littered with references to the attacks on New York on 11 September 2001. The film, of course, is set in New York. As will be seen in the Textual Analysis section the desecration of the Statue of Liberty can be equated with the destruction of the World Trade Center and the smoke billowing down streets recalls scenes from that day. The two skyscrapers from where Beth is rescued are also reminiscent of the Twin Towers of the World Trade Center.

But it is not just the 9/11 attacks that are a strong theme in the film; it is the notion of 'Western anxiety' in general which is explored. 'Western anxiety' might be defined as a deep-seated and contagious unease that will afflict whole nations, and indeed, large parts of the Western world in general. In recent years the main causes of this collective angst have been terrorism consuming the world, bird flu wiping out millions and global warming making earth uninhabitable.

Films can often help people face these fears in a manageable and often exciting way, displacing an audience's real fears and channelling them through entertainment. For terrorists, just get James Bond or John McClane (the *Die Hard* films) to sort them out; films like *Outbreak* (1995), *28 Days Later* (2002) and *Doomesday* (2008) have shown (rather creatively) the effect of viruses; and global warming has been explored in *Waterworld* (1995) and *The Day After Tomorrow* (2004). *Cloverfield* taps into these fears. The monster symbolises the terrorist threat, there is the body horror associated with viruses shown in the effect of being bitten by one of the monster's parasites, and the mass destruction of life echoes the warnings associated with global warming.

SELECT FILMOGRAPHY OF MAIN PRODUCERS AND CAST

Matt Reeves, 1966, Director, Writer, Producer

Film
Future Shock, 1993
The Pallbearer, 1996
Cloverfield, 2008

Television
Felicity, 1998–2001

J. J. Abrams, 1966, Producer, Writer, Director

Film

Regarding Henry, 1991
Forever Young, 1992
The Pallbearer, 1996
The Suburbans, 1999
Joy Ride, 2001
Cloverfield, 2008
Star Trek, 2009

Television

Felicity, 1998-2002
Alias, 2001-2006
What About Brian, 2006–2007
Lost, 2004–present

REPRESENTATION

New York City

New York City has appeared many times as a backdrop to films. A giant ape has gone on the rampage in *King Kong* (1933); there has been a romantic *homage* to a part of the city in *Manhattan* (1979); its violent and criminal underbelly has been exposed in *Mean Streets* (1973) and *Taxi Driver* (1976); it has become a maximum security prison in *Escape from New York* (1981); and more recently it has been decimated by flood and ice in *The Day After Tomorrow* (2004).

New York is a city of iconic sites: the Statue of Liberty, Central Park, the Empire State Building and the Brooklyn Bridge, to name but a few. *Cloverfield* taps into the significance of some of these sites. They are symbols that carry great resonance throughout the world, particularly the Statue of Liberty with its connotations of freedom, democracy and people's dreams of success. For American audiences in particular the pre-footage caption, stating that the digital film file was found in an area formerly known as Central Park, would carry a chilling echo of what happened to their beloved city when it was attacked in 2001.

New York is the most well-known of all American cities across the globe, more so even than the capital Washington D.C. It represents both the epitome of the American Dream and the dark underbelly of crime and poverty, home to success and failure in equal measure. In *Cloverfield* the destruction brings a democracy of despair to New Yorkers. Everyone (rich, poor, black, white) is under threat and this found digital file, coupled with the final images of bombardment, suggest that even a great city like New York cannot be certain of its future.

Twenty-somethings

The first 15 minutes of *Cloverfield* explores middle-class, often white, men and women in their twenties. Contemporary North American television has been dominated by such characters, and has been particularly influential in creating programmes featuring the trials and tribulations of young adults. The sitcom *Friends* (1994–2004) was instrumental in creating a focus on these sorts of characters, with more (melo)dramatic examples being *Party of Five* (1994–2000), *Dawson's Creek* (1998–2003) and *The O.C.* (2003–2007). Other television programmes, from which *Cloverfield* would seem to have drawn its inspiration, include shows such as *Buffy The Vampire Slayer* (1997–2003), Abrams' own *Lost* and *Heroes* (2006–present). All combine young adult themes with supernatural plotlines inflected by the science fiction and horror genres.

In the first part of *Cloverfield* the young group of 20-somethings deal with typical issues. There is a secret relationship between a young man and a friend (just as Chandler and Monica or Ross and Rachel get together in *Friends*), a relationship complicated by the fact that he is leaving to work in Japan, while the film's main cameraman, Hud, tries desperately to make conversation with the girl of his dreams, Marlena. This depiction of casually affluent young New Yorkers caught up in typical relationship scenarios is familiar to young audiences and makes the sudden destruction by the monster of this plotline all the more jarring and effective.

Actors

The main actors in *Cloverfield* are all relatively unknown, particularly outside of the United States and in terms of film work. They could be all described as up and coming actors who are in their early to late twenties, a group that a young audience can relate to. Michael Stahl-David has some television experience but this was his biggest role to date, as is the case with the other main actors, particularly T.J. Miller, Odette Yustman and Jessica Lucas. Lizzy Caplan had appeared in a supporting role in 2004's *Mean Girls*, starring Lindsay Lohan, but it is Mike Vogel who has had most film exposure, with roles in *The Texas Chainsaw Massacre* (2003) and *Poseidon* (2006). Undoubtedly, the use of relatively unknown faces in *Cloverfield* helps add authenticity to the premise that this is footage recovered from the scene of the attack in New York.

TEXTUAL ANALYSIS

The first attack (DVD Chapters 4 & 5, 0:16:40)

Summary

Jason decides to have a heart-to-heart conversation with his brother, Rob, about his recent sexual encounter with mutual friend, Beth. The conversation is interrupted by what appears to be an earthquake tremor. After going up to the roof to investigate, explosions and flying debris send the partygoers and all their neighbours on to the streets, where they witness the collapse of skyscrapers and the head of the Statue of Liberty crashing to the ground. The street then becomes full of smoke whilst the main protagonists hide in a shop and some *thing* – they do not know what – passes close by. Outside there is a scene of devastation and confusion.

Camerawork

As with *The Blair Witch Project* (1999), the camerawork is intended to imitate a home video with all its flaws (shaky, whip pans and fast zooms, for example) suggesting that the footage is 'real'. Domestic camcorders are now so commonplace that audiences have a connection with this sort of footage; it charts people's lives and now often records world events, its shaky capturing of events, such as the attack on the World Trade Center, giving the images a frightening immediacy. *Cloverfield* attempts to mimic these real-life images and, indeed, there are some direct parallels with the footage from that day.

The opening conversation between Jason and his brother contains some of the few static shots in the film, which reinforce the impact of the tremor that initiates the destruction of the city. The camera is also tilted, indicating

101

that, although they are having a very normal conversation about relationships, there is a degree of unease. Another aspect of this scene is the framing of the two men. As they are out on a small fire escape there is a confined and claustrophobic sense to the frame, which adds to the sense of unease, but there is also a fairly large space between the two men. The gap subtly suggests a degree of uncertainty and perhaps threat. The framing becomes tighter on Rob as the conversation gets more heated about his relationship with Beth, and the increasingly tight framing of his face underpins the intensity of this personal trauma. The focus on this micro drama ensures that the shift to the macro issue, the rampaging monster, is all the more startling and unexpected.

After the tremor the camerawork becomes more jerky as

confusion takes hold of the partygoers. However, it is not until some of them go onto the roof and witness the enormous explosion that the camerawork becomes frenetic, fully submerging the audience into events. As Hud and the others run from the falling debris, it is as much about what we do not see as what we do that is frightening for the audience. In the mayhem the camera imitates the frenzied panic of the populace, even blacking out at times; in this way it mimics an individual's perspective on events, uncomprehending and terrified.

The sequence in the street and in the shop continues to

capture the sense of reality, also known as verisimilitude, an eyewitness account of events beyond the individual's control. As the head of the Statue of Liberty hurtles towards the camera the audience shares the bystanders' alarm. The camera initially zooms in on the statue and the audience focuses on the alarming gouges in its face. The audience's full realisation of the identity of the object is further delayed as we wait for the camera to zoom out, thus increasing our sense of anticipation.

As the camera crouches with the characters in the shop, the audience feels their sense of disorientation and fear. The camera's continual jerky movements, nervously peering from behind the shelves, suggest the feeling that we too are being hunted.

 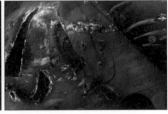

This sort of camerawork is not unique to *Cloverfield* or *The Blair Witch Project*; many films have moments of handheld camera movement, particularly at times of extreme confusion or action. The opening battle scene to *Saving Private Ryan* (1998) is an excellent example of this style of film-making. Often, a handheld camera can be used to convey a character's point of view (POV), a device used in *Saving Private Ryan* as a soldier disembarks a landing craft during the Normandy landings of 1944 in the Second World War.

Film-makers have long strived to make the action as 'real' as possible, shooting in a style to give the action a sense of verisimilitude. For example, the Italian neo-realist films, such as Roberto Rossilini's *Rome: Open City* (1945), tried to achieve a documentary feel to their films, attempting to plunge the audience into the experiences of post-war Italy by using unfamiliar, often war-ravaged, real-life locations rather than studio sets.

Sound

As a piece of 'real' video footage there is only non-diegetic sound; everything heightens the audience's experience of the terrifying events depicted in this scene. Once the explosion has occurred there are numerous examples of overlapping dialogue which helps accentuate the sense of confusion and individual disorientation. There is a cacophony of sound: explosions, screams and alarms erupt as the characters are plunged into a nightmarish world. The screams subside as the hushed tones of wonder, and then perhaps excitement, take over as they rush up to the roof.

Amidst the overlapping dialogue, a woman's voice rings out, 'do you think it's another terrorist attack?' It is one of many references, particularly of the visual kind, to the 9/11 attacks on New York. Hud's laboured breathing helps draw the audience into the sense of expectation as the characters arrive on the apartment block's roof to catch a glimpse of the devastation.

The sound of sirens punctures the night air and emphasises the atmosphere of danger. We also hear a male voice saying 'terrorist attack', adding to the sense of threat. This is almost immediately followed by a massive explosion, which also taps into this idea of a terrorist attack. Although the sound of the explosion is somewhat muted, as it comes from some distance away, it is the sound of the debris flying through the air that signals that catastrophe is fast approaching. Again, shouts, screams, explosions, alarms and the fracturing of the camera sound, as the debris crashes into the apartment and Hud falls to the ground, underpin the chaotic scene.

Outside, there is a cacophony of shouts and screams as people flee from the destruction; it is the sound of panic and fear. The sounds of the Statue of Liberty's head flying through the air and crashing against a building increase the sense of terror that the people on the street experience as they react to this fast-approaching danger. The destruction caused by the head and its immense weight is underlined by the sound of its metal shell screeching and groaning as it comes to rest on the street; the shouts and screams of disbelief add to the fear and surreal nature of the moment. The continuing sound of alarms underpins the unsettling atmosphere, as does the chorus of frightened voices.

There is no let-up in the diegetic sound and we hear, before seeing, the next threat which adds to our, and the onscreen characters', sense of fearful expectation. The low and deep noise of an unearthly growling is mixed with the sound of the ground being thudded, as well as falling rubble from the destroyed building. Again, the people's screams as they run from the dust clouds maintain the sense of fear. From within the shop where the characters take refuge the outside sounds of twisting metal, falling debris and guttural growls help to sustain the menace of the as-yet-unseen creature.

In the shop the thunderous thuds, the falling stock from the shelves and the individual screams are mixed with the main characters' frightened and hushed words to create a palpable sense of dislocation and abject fear. The complete change to almost silence once the creature has moved on is a sharp contrast to the noise of the scene so far and the sounds of alarms and coughing outside underpin the eerie atmosphere created by the dust clouds. These sparing sounds also emphasise the surreal nature of the immediate post-attack scene, one where confusion reigns, just like the aftermath of a bomb attack to which this scene is clearly linked in terms of its combined use of sound and visuals.

Editing

The editing of the scene follows the conventions of continuity editing; we see the narrative unfolding in a sequence of events typical of Hollywood films. However, in keeping with what we might expect of amateur video footage, there are cuts in the action to indicate that the camera has stopped and restarted. Sometimes, such as when the characters are running up and down the stairwell of the apartment block, there are significant cuts. In traditional film-making these would be known as jump cuts and they are used to create a jarring effect, which adds to the sense of dislocation.

Jump cuts were extensively used in the late 1950s and 1960s by French film directors, otherwise known as the French New Wave. Jean-Luc Godard's *Breathless* (1960) employs jump cuts at moments in the film when there is intense action, such as when a policeman is shot. Although the effect of removing key visual information can disorientate the audience, in this way we become more involved in the chaotic and disturbing action. For the rest of the scene there is only one more clear cut, just after the descent to street level (there may be one or two hidden cuts in the shop when the lights go out and after the explosion which blows out the windows). With the continuous running of footage this scene of high drama can be 'lived' by the audience as they are drawn into its intensely 'real' atmosphere, uninterrupted by the use of editing.

Mise-en-scène

The mise-en-scène in the opening part of the film is designed to create a sense of normality and reality; it is a party full of young people, in their twenties in a large Manhattan apartment. The guests are a mixed group of fairly affluent-looking people, suggested by their mode of dress, as well as the fact that they are trendy and generally high achievers. This sense of normality ensures that the tremor and explosion are all the more shocking for the audience as we see this everyday world shaken and familiar places and objects destroyed. This emphasis on the ordinary imbues the action with its sense of reality, as if this is home video footage, as well as recalling countless news images from battles across the world, images which often come from cities wrecked by army or guerrilla bombardment.

Other key elements of the mise-en-scène include the use of smoke and dust as it pours down the streets following the collapse of buildings. It is an image particularly reminiscent of eyewitness video footage of the streets around the World Trade Center following their collapse after the 9/11 attacks. This aspect of the mise-en-scène generates a resonance for all viewers who have seen those images, charging it with a great deal of poignancy. The film-makers' decision to include these shots can be interpreted as a way of signalling the film's attempts to connect with post-9/11 paranoia and a universal sense of unpredictable threat. This, in turn, can be seen as either a legitimate and effective strategy or a blatant attempt to feed off real images of disaster, which some may consider rather offensive and an example of unimaginative film-making.

The Statue of Liberty is a very potent symbol both for Americans and the rest of the world; it symbolises the ideal of America itself with the figure, torch and book representing freedom, enlightenment and knowledge. This iconic image is probably the most recognisable structure associated with the United States; for many, it is the United States and everything that it would like to uphold, notably democracy and freedom. It has stood in its position on Liberty Island in New York Harbour since 1886, and was also a powerful image for the millions of immigrants who would arrive by boat to New York dreaming of new beginnings and success.

In films this symbolism has been used in various ways: it stood as that of immigrants' dreams in *The Godfather II* (1974), whilst in the earlier *Planet of the Apes* (1968) its apparent destruction is shocking evidence of humanity's inclination to self-destruct. A frozen Statue of Liberty is prominent in *The Day After Tomorrow*, a symbol of civilisation coming to an end. This subversion of the iconic image was also used in the poster campaign for *Escape from New York* (1981), an action/ science fiction film set in 1997 in which Manhattan Island has been turned into a maximum security prison where inmates are left to fend for themselves; Liberty Island acts as base for the police guarding the prison.

The poster shows the head of the statue lying in a street and helps emphasise the underlying message of moral decay in American society, both in the criminals and in the military/ government (the establishment). J.J. Abrams has said that his inspiration for the use of the Statue of Liberty's head comes from this film, and indeed, the sight of the disembodied head is very disorientating and quite shocking, particularly for American viewers. The way it unceremoniously bounces off buildings and down the street and comes to rest in the middle of the road signals that whatever has done this is no respecter of tradition and iconography. The sinister gouges in its face are further evidence that this American icon has been defiled. This again links to the images from the attacks on the World Trade Center, the two iconic buildings that actually were destroyed that day.

A final aspect of the mise-en-scène is the use of mobile phones after the Statue of Liberty's head has landed in the street; the first reaction of the bystanders is to record the image of the head. This seems to be the modern reaction to events; it almost seems that if an event or emotion is not recorded then it has not properly existed. It is the sort of modern condition revealed in such programmes as *The Jerry Springer Show*, *Big Brother* or any of the countless reality shows that inhabit the television channels.

As well as the filming of spectacular events, there are numerous moments of close-up self-revelation by the characters, either direct to camera or filmed in documentary style by Hud, where we hear their innermost thoughts (the filming of Rob's argument with Beth, Jason's heart-to-heart with Rob, and the final messages from Rob and Beth, both in Central Park and on Coney Island for example). In this way the audience taps into people's lives in the same manner as they do in reality shows and the hand-held intimate quality of the camerawork adds to the verisimilitude of the images. Indeed, some of these monologues and dialogues, particularly earlier on in the film, could be lifted straight out of the Jeremy Kyle Show with their emphasis on love and sex.

Colour and lighting

For most of this scene the colours are quite muted, with lots of browns, blacks and dark oranges. This adds a downbeat atmosphere to the scene and acts as a contrast to the dramatic explosions bursting with light. These dark colours and the clouds of choking dust help mirror the catastrophic events, as if something hellish will emerge from the darkness. The only other burst of colour, apart from the explosions, is in the interior of the shop with its brightly-lit merchandise on the shelves. It is a brief moment of vivid and rich colour, representing normality and life, until that too is plunged into darkness and then it is drained of all colour once the windows have exploded and the dust has entered the building as the creature passes along the street outside.

Again, as the film is trying to imitate an amateur's video footage of a real event the lighting is designed to be naturalistic. The scene has of course been carefully lit, but only to appear as if it is real and unlit! This imbues the scene with verisimilitude and helps create a sense of real events unfolding. As the camera is thrust around the apartment building the lighting is erratic, plunging from brightness to darkness, Hud's fall on the stairs and in the shop signalling moments of blind terror.

As it is night time the lighting, once outside, has pools of darkness amidst the streetlights and failing electricity (due to the explosions), which also adds to the terror and mounting chaos. The only strongly-lit place is the shop where Hud and some others take cover. Its bright, artificial lighting is a contrast to the murkiness of the street, and its flickering and failure as the monster approaches makes this part of the scene all the more unsettling.

'Godzilla meets YouTube... *Cloverfield*'s brilliantly simple gimmick is to take a traditional monster movie scenario and shoot the carnage from ground up, using a single camcorder carried by one of the protagonists... *Cloverfield* is the monster movie as seen from the point of view of the innocent bystander. It succeeds brilliantly in reconciling its camcorder *vérité* style with the traditional demands of a big blockbuster. So, there are the usual character arcs and an appreciable three act structure, but they're craftily concealed within the chaotic rush of "found" footage.

This is actually rather comforting, since the scenes of destroyed buildings and panicked crowds have a whiff of authenticity that edges the movie into allegorical territory - it's 9/11 with a big-ass troll-lizard beastie instead of terrorists... *Cloverfield* feels like a nightmare dredged up from the 21st century subconscious.'

Paul Arendt, *BBCi*, 01 February 2008

Chapter 6: Parody and Reality – *Airplane!* and *United 93*

Airplane!

KEY FACTS

Release Date: 1980

Country of Origin: USA

Running Time: 84 minutes

Budget

$3,500,000

PRODUCTION NOTES

Production Company

Paramount Pictures

Distributor

Paramount Pictures

Marketing – Taglines

You've read the ad, now see the movie!

A typically direct and comic marketing ploy undercutting the usual Hollywood dramatic hype when trying to entice audiences to see a film. Just as the film deconstructs the disaster genre, and others, so the advertising makes fun of... advertising.

What's slower than a speeding bullet, and able to hit tall buildings at a single bound?

Thank God it's Only a Motion Picture!

The craziest flight you'll ever take!

The Plane's going to Chicago. The Pilot's going to New York. The Passengers are going to Pieces!

The first of these is in hindsight a rather unfortunate tagline considering the events of 9/11, 20 years later, but all four are typical of the film's deadpan and offbeat humour, acknowledging its absurdity and feeding this into its marketing campaign.

Poster

"Something hit us... the crew is dead... help us, please, please help us!"

AIRPORT 1975

An all *NEW* motion picture event-inspired by the novel "AIRPORT" by Arthur Hailey.

CHARLTON HESTON
KAREN BLACK · GEORGE KENNEDY · GLORIA SWANSON
EFREM ZIMBALIST JR. · SUSAN CLARK · SID CAESAR · LINDA BLAIR · DANA ANDREWS
ROY THINNES · NANCY OLSON · ED NELSON · MYRNA LOY · AUGUSTA SUMMERLAND and HELEN REDDY

FLIGHT 23 CRASHES IN BERMUDA TRIANGLE...PASSENGERS ALIVE, TRAPPED UNDERWATER...

AIRPORT '77 ALL NEW!

A JENNINGS LANG PRODUCTION
JACK LEMMON
LEE GRANT · BRENDA VACCARO · JOSEPH COTTEN · OLIVIA de HAVILLAND
DARREN McGAVIN · CHRISTOPHER LEE · GEORGE KENNEDY
JAMES STEWART as Phillip Stevens

The picture on the *Airplane!* poster underlines the offbeat and zany humour of the film with the aircraft tied up in knots, but it also links to the images on the posters for the *Airport* series of films. Each one shows an aircraft in a position of danger and the *Airplane* poster taps into the increasing absurdity of the scenarios of the *Airport* films.

Synopsis

Elaine is an air-stewardess and Ted, an ex-fighter pilot, is on board her flight in an attempt to win back the girl he loves. Ted takes over the controls when its crew and some of its passengers are stricken with food poisoning. As well as the events on board and at the airport we also see flashbacks of Ted and Elaine's romantic relationship. Ultimately, Ted manages to land the plane safely and the couple are happy together again.

Commentary

The 1970s' disaster film cycle was running out of steam by the end of the decade; judging by box office returns, audiences could only cope with so many films of this sort. While budgets and the quality of casts had remained high, films such as *The Towering Inferno* retained some credibility. But the formula quickly became riddled with clichéd plots and characters and films in the late 1970s pitted a range of stars against ever-more unlikely disaster scenarios: Michael Caine battled against killer bees in *The Swarm* (1978) and was also on board the tired sequel, *Return to the Poseidon Adventure* (1979). Irwin Allen had lost his magic touch. But even these unsuccessful bigger budget films seemed like masterworks when compared to the plethora of B-movie imitators that were made in this period, including *Flood!* (1976) and *City on Fire* (1979).

There had always been something laughable about the big stars' heroics in these films (see Dean Martin in *Airport*), and the dialogue sometimes creaked under the weight of its own banality. When one looks at *Airport* it is clear to see where the makers of *Airplane!* got their inspiration.

The Western is another genre that has become beset by routine plots and clichéd dialogue over the years, and the 'a man's gotta do what a man's gotta do' stereotype has been the subject of parody for many years. Films such as *Destry Rides Again* (1939), *Annie Get Your Gun* (1950), *Cat Ballou* (1965) and, most notably, *Blazing Saddles* (1974), have all exploited the codes and conventions of the genre for comic effect.

Airplane! announces its comic intentions from the opening credits with its parody of *Jaws* (1975) through its use of similar music and the visuals of the plane's tail cutting through the clouds like a shark's fin in the water. There are parodic references to numerous other films throughout, including the disco dancing scene from *Saturday Night Fever* (1977) and the beach kissing scene in *From Here To Eternity* (1953). But the disaster film, in particular, is the film's chief source material; the opening titles are reminiscent of those in *Airport* with their big bold text, as are the visuals of airport life and the grand orchestral score. There is, of course, the 'flight in peril' storyline that comes from *Airport*, but every character stereotype and clichéd line is used from that film and subverted for comic effect.

Just as in *Airport* there is a nun on board and a slapping incident, with all the passengers queuing up to inflict pain on the hysterical woman. The plot and lines of dialogue are borrowed from the CBS television film *Flight Into Danger* (1956) and directly parody *Zero Hour!* (1957) as well as elements of *Airport 1975*. There are numerous other references to disaster films to add to the audience's enjoyment. They include casting Kareem Abdul-Jabbar, a famous basketball player, to connect with the casting of O.J. Simpson, the celebrated American football player (more recently, the infamous participant in an armed robbery) who had earlier appeared in *The Towering Inferno*. Also, Robert Stack (Captain Rex Kramer) appeared as an airline captain in *The High and the Mighty* (1954), a film charting a plane flight that gets into difficulty after engine failure. Its all-star cast and lengthy flashback sequences also help link it to *Airplane!*.

As in many disaster films the main characters are given some backstory so that the audience can identify with them, particularly when their lives are in danger. Ted Striker is given a ridiculous history whereby the flashbacks to his air force days are obviously absurd as we see images of World War Two, events which would have happened before Striker was born. Elaine Dickinson, stewardess and object of Striker's affection, is shown to be living in Drambuie (an alcoholic drink, not actually a place) on the Barbary Coast (the north and western part of the African coastline synonymous with piracy and kidnapping in previous centuries); again, the couple's presence there and the events of their disco dancing meeting are comically absurd.

Other characters on the plane and at the airport develop the disaster film convention of having a disparate group of characters brought together. But for each one there is a twist to their personality to undermine the stereotype. There is the sensible captain (whose behaviour is rather bizarre), the chief at the airport who starts off in control of the situation and then becomes side-tracked with glue-sniffing, the seemingly kind old lady (who kills herself rather than listen to Striker's life story), the children (who carry out a rather mature courtship), the sick child (whose intravenous drip is accidentally pulled out by the singing stewardess for comic effect), and the Afro-American men whose jive talk is parodied.

Once the familiar disaster plot is underway the device of food poisoning leading to the crew's and passengers' ill-health allows for a number of conventions to be parodied and subverted. The mentally-scarred Striker comes forward as the only hope (the fire chief in *The Towering Inferno* or the priest in *The Poseidon Adventure* are typical examples of this character type). He must overcome his feelings of fear and guilt (he believes that it was his fault that fellow airman died during the war) to fly the plane. The convention of panicking passengers is parodied when they are told that there is no pilot and the ensuing chaos contains shots of a barebreasted woman, a fighting nun and two swordfighting men.

During moments of 'tension' the dramatic music underscores the comic dialogue: 'Mr. Striker, I know nothing about flying, but there's one thing I do know: you're the only one on this plane who can possibly fly it. You're the only chance we've got.' Clichés like this are plentiful in the script and link the film to similar dialogue in straightforward disaster films, further subverting the genre. It is not so much the crashing of the plane but the comic insensitivity of the crew that imperils the passengers' mental health: stewardess Elaine asks if anyone can fly a plane, whilst the other, Randy, shows them their lifejacket which is an inflatable duck. The fact that the in-flight film depicts an aircraft crashing just adds to the comic escalation of peril that the passengers must be feeling.

The dramatic climax where Striker saves the day and lands the plane also mimics the disaster film ending. However, the convention is undermined by a number of images: his profuse sweating which looks like gushing water; the emergency vehicles followed by a beer truck, an ice-cream van and a cement mixing lorry amongst others; the waiting people who have to run from gate to gate as the crashlanding plane hurtles along the runway. Even the convention of seeing the characters reach safety is comically subverted by the stewardess' cheerful words ('Have a nice day. Thank you for travelling Trans American') to the distraught passengers as they leap down the inflated escape chute, and by the crashing ambulance containing the young girl.

The final convention of having some romantic attachment is adhered to courtesy of Striker and Elaine, but their final kissing moment is undermined by the hysterical non-diegetic singing and Otto, the inflatable auto-pilot, who pilots the plane back into the air and is revealed to have a female inflatable companion. It is them and the departing plane that the audience see last, not the human couple.

Thus, in many ways *Airplane!* adheres to the main conventions of the disaster film: the disruption to the equilibrium with the food poisoning narrative; a hero; romance; threat; a mixed group of characters (some with backstories); children; tension (albeit comic); an expert (Captain Kramer); and a cast (Leslie Nielsen, Robert Stack, Lloyd Bridges) who collectively had appeared in many Hollywood films from the 1930s onwards and who would have been well-known to older audiences, if not to the teenagers who flocked to see the film. It is from its playful subversion of these conventions that much of the humour in the film is derived.

SELECT FILMOGRAPHY OF MAIN PRODUCERS AND CAST

Jim Abrahams, 1944

David Zucker, 1947

Jerry Zucker, 1950, Directors, Writers, Producers

Airplane!, 1980
Top Secret!, 1984
Ruthless People, 1986
The Naked Gun series (1988–94)

'For audiences increasingly tired with the pompous 70s disaster movies that merely recycled former glories, *Airplane!* was the key that unlocked them from the shackles of big budget boredom. The relentless stream of gags, many at the expense of glossy Hollywood dramas, were unflinching in exposing contrived plot devices to maximum comedic effect. www.bbc.uk/films

'...*Airplane!* is practically a satirical anthology of classic movie clichés. Lloyd Bridges, as the ground-control officer, seems to be satirizing half of his straight roles. The opening titles get an enormous laugh with an unexpected reference to *Jaws*. The neurotic young pilot is talked back into the cockpit in a scene from *Knute Rockne, All American*. And the romantic scenes are played as a soap opera. None of this really adds up to great comic artistry, but *Airplane!* compensates for its lack of original comic invention by its utter willingness to steal, beg, borrow, and rewrite from anywhere.' Roger Ebert, 7 May, 1980

United 93

KEY FACTS

Release Date: 2006

Country of Origin: UK

Running Time: 106 minutes

Budget

$15,000,000

PRODUCTION NOTES

Production Companies

Working Title Films

Universal Pictures

Studio Canal

Sidney Kimmel
Entertainment

Distributor

Universal Pictures

Marketing – Taglines

On September 11 Four Planes Were Hijacked. Three Hit Their Targets. One Did Not.

> The tagline is clear and direct; it is factual, but also dramatic enough to hook the audience. There is so much

public knowledge and interest in the events of that day that there is no need to put too much of a Hollywood gloss on its marketing campaign. Also, the fact that it is an event that continues to be connected with such powerful emotions means that there is a certain amount of sensitivity for the victims' families and friends.

On September 11th, one of the darkest days in our history, 40 ordinary people sat down as strangers, and stood up as one.

The war on terror begins with 40 ordinary people.

These two taglines are emotive and strive to connect the audience with the subject matter in a more personal way. The first one uses the word 'our' to increase the emotional impact of the message, namely, that we are all connected to the events of that day. Both taglines also refer to the passengers as 'ordinary people', again to help underline that the film is dealing with a very human and real issue. For American audiences in particular, these taglines would be resonant and stir up great emotions of patriotism and notions of individual and collective acts of heroism.

United they stood.

This is simple and direct, feeding into the idea of the passengers' great struggle and, again, as a statement of the passengers' courage. It is respectful and would appeal to a Western audience's feelings of reverence for these people. Of course, the word 'United' neatly links to the name of the aircraft and the film, *United 93*.

Poster

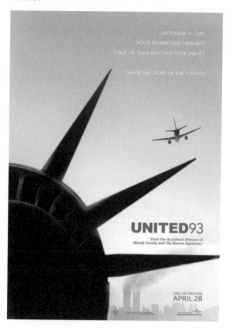

The poster is an emotive picture, full of iconic images from the day of the 9/11 attack. A fragment of the Statue of Liberty can be seen in silhouette, a symbol of justice and freedom to many Americans, and, as we have seen from *Cloverfield*, a shorthand image for the United States itself for people around the world. The fact that it cannot be seen clearly might suggest that this was a day when the very concepts of freedom and justice were also obscured. In the background there is another silhouette, the famous Manhattan skyline, which contains the now iconic image of smoke billowing from the twin towers of the World Trade Center.

Coupled with the image of an aircraft heading in the direction of Manhattan, it is a restrained but potent design capable of stirring up many emotions among the prospective audience, particularly with the American people. Its tagline, 'On September 11 four planes were hijacked. Three of them reached their target. This is the story of the fourth', is simple and direct and does not over dramatise the event, yet it is enigmatic and would help attract its reader to a story of great bravery. Like the film itself, the marketing here is unadorned and without the usual level of Hollywood drama and sentimentality.

The poster above shows a mosaic of faces and the minute details of airport life. In this way it resembles the film's approach in that it has a very naturalistic atmosphere with its documentary-style camerawork and low-key performances. It shows how the extraordinary events occurred on a very ordinary day and how the victims were ordinary people, unknowingly part of a larger picture and united by the aircraft, which is illustrated at the centre of the poster. The colours gradually change from an orange glow at the top to black and white at the bottom. The top colour suggests danger but also vibrancy and life, whilst the monochrome bottom connotes a sombre atmosphere and possibly death.

Synopsis

This is the true story of the United Airlines flight that was hijacked on September 11, 2001. Two of the other planes hijacked on that day hit the Twin Towers of the World Trade Center in New York and another crashed into the Pentagon, but the passengers on Flight 93 were able to overcome the hijackers and force the plane to crash in Pennsylvania before it hit its intended target, believed to be Washington D.C.

Commentary

The events of 11 September, 2001 resonated throughout the world. The shocking images shot by both news channels and members of the public were transmitted into people's homes. It was the images from the latter source that brought a real sense of immediacy to the events, letting viewers right into the heart of the drama in an unprecedented way.

These incidents had come in the wake of many other bomb attacks around the world, but this was the first that had seriously encroached onto American soil. The American people were incredulous that al-Qaeda could strike at the heart of their country with such an audacious and catastrophic attack. The hijackers' plan was reminiscent of a Hollywood film plot, the type of outrageous narrative that was often created by film-makers – only this time it was real. Playing out before the world, this series of events almost defied belief, a disaster film of epic proportions. Almost 3,000 people died on that day and the aftershocks of the events are still felt today. It was followed by attacks in London on 7 July, 2005 with the loss of nearly 60 lives and 700 injuries, as well as the related wars in Iraq and Afghanistan and numerous attacks worldwide.

United 93 is not the only film dealing with events from that day. There are also the television film *Flight 93* (2006) and *World Trade Center* (2006) that follow events in a more conventional Hollywood manner, the latter starring A-list actor Nicolas Cage and employing more traditional Hollywood devices of drama and sentimentality. The difference with *United 93* is its commitment to create a sense of verisimilitude through jerky handheld camerawork, similar to that in *Cloverfield*, mimicking news footage.

Paul Greengrass, its British director, writer and producer had already gained critical praise for his earlier film, *Bloody Sunday* (2002), a retelling of the events in Northern Ireland on 30 January, 1972 when British soldiers shot and killed 14 civil rights protesters. It was another event that made headlines throughout the world and Greengrass again attempted to bring the terror of the events through camerawork that imitated real footage of the day. It is perhaps all the more surprising, with this in mind, that the company behind *United 93* is Working Title, a British-run company that has been responsible for some of the most romantic and less than realistic films of recent times, including *Notting Hill* (1999) and *Wimbledon* (2004).

United 93's commitment to carefully representing actual events is further exemplified by its use in some instances of the actual people, including air traffic controllers, who were working on September 11, as well as having the full backing and support of the passengers' relatives, some of whom received phone calls from those on the flight. Details of these calls add authenticity to the narrative, which, because there were no survivors, must in part be based on conjecture.

But the question is: how does *United 93* fit into the disaster genre? It contains numerous examples of the genre's codes and conventions: a group of people of various ages and backgrounds are brought together on a plane; the flight soon runs into danger with the action of the hijackers; the authorities (the air traffic controllers and the military) try to effect a solution; there is a gradual build-up of tension and the ordinary people on the plane become heroic as they appear to overcome the hijackers.

However, it wears its disaster convention clothes very loosely. There is no getting away from the fact that this is based on actual events, and it's not *any* plane crash; this was part of events that are some of the most significant of recent times, or any times. This heavy burden of actuality makes the events all the more charged and the audience's reaction all the more emotional. Yes, there is tension here, but it is not melodramatic; it is more akin to watching footage of suffering on a news bulletin.

By examining some moments in the film it is possible to see how the disaster film structure is evoked, rather like a ghost in the background. The main protagonists are introduced to the audience, firstly the hijackers, then the crew and finally the passengers. But apart from seeing the hijackers at prayer, there is no backstory for any of the characters and certainly no flashbacks. In this way the characters remain somewhat anonymous in comparison with the fleshed out personalities in traditional genre films. We do not need to know about them;

it is enough to know that these were real people. It is this, coupled with their telephone calls to their friends and families, which adds to the audience's engagement with the characters. Gone is the sentimentality of a typical Hollywood genre film and instead there is a real emotional connection with the plight of the characters.

In *The Poseidon Adventure* and *The Towering Inferno* the plots originate around glamorous events, a New Year Eve's party and a VIP reception respectively, but in *United 93* it is the very ordinariness of the situation, an internal plane flight, which adds poignancy to the film. There is no all-star cast to get in the way of the audience's connection with the events as they unfold. Big star actors or even recognisable faces always carry the baggage of their previous appearances. Here, with the unknown cast, the focus remains on the events. The arrival of the characters is played out in a very low-key manner; we hear only snippets of their conversations and there is no focus on any one character or characters, except for the hijackers, and the ordinary routines of boarding a plane dominate the visuals.

The crashing of the two planes into the World Trade Center is part of the horror of that day and is chillingly played out on the radar screens of the air traffic controllers, on the news footage and from some eyewitness views of the crashes and their aftermath. These events lead up to the focus of the film so that when the hijackers on United 93 finally act there is already a high level of tension. All this is achieved with a documentary-style level of realism, the constantly moving hand-held camera reminiscent of the way that war zone news footage is often captured, a device used in *Cloverfield*.

Another key difference between *United 93* and the more common variety of disaster film is the sense of spectacle. Disaster films will tend to have spectacular action in terms of explosions and devastation, utilising special effects to a large degree. Here the focus on board the plane, the air traffic controllers' centre and the interior of the military base give the film a much more claustrophobic atmosphere, which creates intense emotions rather than relying on sensationalism through spectacular effects.

The audience is certainly drawn into the tension and terror of the action on board the flight, just as it would be in any disaster film. The struggle of the passengers to extricate themselves from the disaster scenario is just as gripping as in any fictional narrative but is rendered even more intense because it is based on real events and by Greengrass' low-key approach. Of course, it is important to note that there is no real way of knowing exactly what happened on the flight and in this way the action is obviously filtered through writer/director Greengrass' visualisation; there is always a degree of Hollywood gloss as all texts are mediated in some way.

There are moments in the film where its director's desire to present an almost documentary vision are compromised by what is shown. As the hijackers travel to the airport there is a glimpse of a sign carrying the inscription 'God Bless America', serving as an ironic contrast to the intentions of the hijackers and perhaps a patriotic aside to reinforce that the film-maker's sympathies lie with the United States. There is also the depiction of the German passenger on board the flight who does not want to use violence against the hijackers but who is overruled by the others. His depiction has been criticised by the man's widow and it seems slightly odd that the only dissenting voice comes from a non-American.

Although disaster films tend to have multiple deaths they are not usually depicted in a very gratuitous manner; indeed there are usually so many deaths that the focus is usually on the spectacle of lots of deaths. In *United 93* the violence seems simultaneously both much more brutally realistic yet unsensationally so. It is more like street violence with all its matter-of-fact horror and suffering, devoid of Hollywood gloss.

The ending, of course, is double-edged. It is a 'victory' for the passengers over the hijackers as they heroically save the flight from reaching its target, believed to be the US Capitol, the building that houses the country's government. However, they are all killed in the act, which does not conform to the disaster film convention of at least some people surviving. It does, however, connect with the idea of the selfless hero, a not uncommon convention. In *The Poseidon Adventure* the priest who leads the group to safety sacrifices himself at the end of the film in order to save the others, while the Bruce Willis character in *Armageddon* does the same to save the earth.

The events of 9/11 have perhaps changed our view of disaster films. Films like *Cloverfield* have tapped into the visuals from the attacks and there is perhaps more of a sense of unease when we look at a disaster film. Although *United 93* shares some fundamental connections with the disaster genre it feels somehow wrong to pass it off simply in those terms. Disaster films have often been seen as dumb spectacle movies whereas *United 93* has more dignity and honesty in its depiction of a very real disaster. As the world becomes increasingly saturated with media texts and the texts themselves are blurring all the time it seems appropriate that a necessarily fictionalised film (for how can we ever know the exact truth of what happened?) about such public events should become part of our collective memory and steer the disaster film into new and uncharted waters.

FILMOGRAPHY OF MAIN PRODUCERS AND CAST

Paul Greengrass, 1955, Director, Writer, Producer

The Theory of Flight, 1998
The Murder of Stephen Lawrence, 1999
Bloody Sunday, 2002
The Bourne Supremacy, 2004
United 93, 2006
The Bourne Ultimatum, 2007
Green Zone, 2009

'What we go through again with the controllers is the gradual apprehension of the unspeakable, unprecedented horror of what is afoot. They haven't had a hijacking for years. With the passengers and crew on Flight 93, we re-experience the discovery that we're living with a new kind of enemy. This isn't one of those hijackings where the perpetrators are seeking a ransom or a flight to freedom. On the ground, the technicians are fumbling to adjust themselves to the beginning of a new era. As at Pearl Harbor, they're unprepared and confused, talking about 'rules of engagement' and discovering that there's nothing they can do until word comes from the President who, like the Vice-President, is incommunicado. The movie manages to be lucid in its presentation of chaos.

It has been said that too little time has passed between the actual events of 9/11 and the making of this docudrama. I cannot agree. Greengrass, his cast and associates have consulted the families of the victims at all stages of making the picture, and they have produced a sober, unsensational film that is at once dramatically involving and morally challenging.' Philip French, *The Observer*, June 4 2006

'This is an Anti-*Titanic* for the multiplexes - a real-life disaster movie with no Leo and Kate and no survivors: only terrorists whose emotional lives are relentlessly blank, and heroes with no backstory...

The director is able to exploit the remarkable fact that the sequence of events, from the first plane crashing into the World Trade Center at a quarter to nine, to the fourth plane ditching into a field in Shanksville, Pennsylvania, at three minutes past 10, fits with horrible irony inside conventional feature-film length, and he is able to unfold the story in real time... the first scenes in which the United 93 passengers enter the plane for their dull, routine early-morning flight are almost unwatchable. These passengers are quite unlike the cross-section of America much mocked in *Airplane!* – with the singing nun and the cute kid – neither are they vividly drawn individuals with ingeniously imagined present or future interconnections, like the cast of TV's *Lost*. They are just affluent professionals from pretty much the same caste, with no great interest in each other, and nothing in common except their fate. And all these people are ghosts, all of them dead men and dead women walking. When they are politely asked to pay attention to the "safety" procedures, ordinary pre-9/11 reality all but snaps in two under the weight of historical irony.'

Peter Bradshaw, *The Guardian*, June 2 2006

Appendix: Creating Your Own Disaster Film

Here are 20 disaster films from the past 25 years with their title, plot synopsis, stars and taglines to help identify some of the conventions needed when putting together a disaster film of your own. Although some of them can easily be defined as belonging to particular genres they all share the 'people-under-threat' convention that is a prominent feature of the disaster film.

Alive (1993)

Plot synopsis:

An Uruguayan aircraft crash lands in the Andes and the survivors resort to eating the remains of their dead fellow passengers to survive. Based on a true story.

Stars:

Ethan Hawke (Nando Parrado)

Taglines:

They survived the impossible... by doing the unthinkable.

They were ordinary young men driven to the very limits of human endurance.

The triumph of the human spirit.

Apollo 13 (1995)

Plot synopsis:

A NASA mission to the moon is threatened when a technical fault cripples the spacecraft and scientists on the ground and the astronauts on board combine to bring them safely back to earth. Based on a real incident.

Stars:

Tom Hanks (Jim Lovell)

Kevin Bacon (Jack Swigert)

Bill Paxton (Fred Haise)

Tagline:

Houston, we have a problem.

Outbreak (1995)

Plot synopsis:

A deadly virus, thought to have been eradicated from Africa in the late 1960s, resurfaces and is brought to the United States by an infected monkey.

Stars:

Dustin Hoffman (Col. Sam Daniels)

Morgan Freeman (Brig. Gen. Billy Ford)

Kevin Spacey (Maj. Casey Schuler)

Cuba Gooding Jr. (Maj. Salt)

Renee Russo (Robby Keough)

Taglines:

Try to remain calm.

This animal carries a deadly virus... and the greatest medical crisis in the world is about to happen.

Independence Day (1996)

Plot synopsis:

Aliens attack the earth but are eventually defeated by fighter pilot Will

Smith and a nuclear bomb planted in the aliens' mothership.

Stars:

Will Smith (Capt. Steven Hiller)

Bill Pullman (President Thomas J. Whitmore)

Jeff Goldblum (David Levinson)

Taglines:

We've always believed we weren't alone. Pretty soon, we'll wish we were.

THESE extraterrestrials don't want to phone home...They want OUR home.

On July 2nd, they arrive. On July 3rd, they strike. On July 4th, we fight back.

Daylight (1996)

Plot synopsis:

Emergency expert Sylvester Stallone rescues some of the survivors from a massive explosion in New York tunnel caused by some thieves crashing into trucks carrying toxic waste.

Star:

Sylvester Stallone (Kit Latura)

Taglines:

Hold your breath.

No air. No escape. No time. No hope.

They went in alone. The only way out is... together !

Twister (1996)

Plot synopsis:

Storm chaser Jo Harding is reunited with her estranged husband, Bill, a fellow meteorologist, whilst trying to launch a new scientific device into a tornado in competition with another group of storm chasers.

Stars:

Helen Hunt (Dr. Jo Harding)

Bill Paxton (Bill Harding)

Taglines:

The Dark Side of Nature.

Don't Breathe. Don't Look Back.

Go for a ride you'll never forget!

Titanic (1997)

Plot synopsis:

Lowly Jack has a whirlwind romance with upper class Rose, much to her boyfriend's irritation; sex, theft and gunfire follow until their story is overtaken by the tragedy of the famous ship's sinking.

Stars:

Leonardo Di Caprio (Jack Dawson)

Kate Winslet (Rose DeWitt Bukater)

Billy Zane (Cal Hockley)

Taglines:

A woman's heart is a deep ocean of secrets.

Nothing On Earth Could Come Between Them.

Anaconda (1997)

Plot synopsis:

A documentary camera crew searching for a lost tribe in South America find a seemingly lost snake hunter who says he can help them. Instead, he has other motives and leads them on a hunt for a gigantic anaconda.

Stars:

Jennifer Lopez (Terri Flores)

Ice Cube (Danny Rich)

Jon Voigt (Paul Sarone)

Taglines:

You can't scream if you can't breathe.

It's a SCREAM!

Dante's Peak (1997)

Plot synopsis:

Volcanologist Harry Dalton goes to the town of Dante's Peak in Washington State to investigate some unusual volcanic activity. There is an eruption, killing numerous people, and Dalton and mayor Rachel Windo with her two children become trapped in a mine shaft...

Stars:

Pierce Brosnan (Harry Dalton)

Linda Hamilton (Rachel Wando)

Taglines:

The pressure is building...

Whatever you do, don't look back.

Armageddon (1998)

Plot synopsis

An asteroid is heading for earth and must be diverted if the human race is to survive; drilling expert Harry Stamper leads a team into space to land on the asteroid.

Stars:

Bruce Willis (Harry J. Stamper)

Billy Bob Thornton (Dan Truman)

Ben Affleck (A.J. Frost)

Liv Tyler (Grace Stamper)

Taglines:

Earth. It Was Fun While It Lasted.

The Earth's Darkest Day Will Be Man's Finest Hour.

Prepare to Fight Like There's No Tomorrow.

Time To Kick Some Asteroid.

Deep Blue Sea (1999)

Plot synopsis:

Susan McCallister, a research scientist, and her team have engineered some genetically modified sharks in order to find a cure for Alzheimer's disease in their aquatic laboratory. The sharks become super-intelligent and start attacking the humans, killing them one by one.

Stars:

Thomas Jane (Carter Blake)

Saffron Burrows (Dr Susan McCallister)

LL Cool J (Sherman 'Preacher' Dudley)

Morgan Freeman (Russell Franklin)

Taglines:

Bigger. Smarter. Faster. Meaner.

Welcome to the endangered species list.

Your worst fear is about to surface.

Lake Placid (1999)

Plot synopsis:

An isolated lake in the state of Maine is terrorised by a giant crocodile; palaeontologist Kelly West and warden Jack Wells join forces to try to capture the creature.

Stars:

Bill Pullman (Jack Wells)

Bridget Fonda (Kelly Scott)

Taglines:

You'll never know what bit you.

Part Mystery Part Thriller Parts Missing.

28 Days Later (2002)

Plot synopsis:

Bicycle courier Jim awakes from a coma to discover that London is seemingly deserted. It soon becomes apparent that a deadly manufactured virus has been unleashed on the public causing its victims to attack others and turn them into zombie-like beings.

Star:

Cillian Murphy (Jim)

His fear began when he woke up alone. His terror began when he realised he wasn't.

Day 1: Exposure - Day 3: Infection - Day 8: Epidemic - Day 15: Evacuation - Day 20: Devastation.

The Days Are Numbered.

Eight Legged Freaks (2002)

Plot synopsis:

Gigantic mutant spiders run riot in a small town after some toxic waste spills into a swamp. A group of townspeople battle to destroy them.

Stars:

David Arquette (Chris McCormick)

Scarlett Johansson (Ashley Parker)

Taglines:

Do you hate spiders? Do you really hate spiders? Well they don't like you either.

Let the squashing begin!!

The biggest... nastiest... mutant spider movie of all time!!!!

The Core (2003)

Plot synopsis:

A plan to extract energy from the earth's core goes awry when it becomes obvious that the planet's rotation is beginning to stop, which will result in the earth becoming open to destruction from the sun's rays. A group journey towards the earth's core to try and save the day.

Stars:

Aaron Eckhart (Dr. Josh Keyes)

Hilary Swank (Maj. Rebecca Childs)

Taglines:

Earth has a deadline.

The only way out is in.

This Spring, Mankind's Greatest Threat Is Earth Itself.

War of the Worlds (2005)

Plot synopsis:

Aliens invade the earth and cause mass destruction and death, with the focus on dock worker Ray Ferrier's struggle to keep himself and his children alive.

Stars:

Tom Cruise (Ray Ferrier)

Dakota Fanning (Rachel)

Tim Robbins (Ogilvy)

Taglines:

They're already here.

This Summer, the last war on Earth won't be started by humans.

Poseidon (2006)

Plot synopsis:

After a rogue wave hits an ocean liner and causes it to capsize a small group of passengers fight their way through a variety of hazards to the hull of the ship and safety.

Stars:

Kurt Russell (Robert Ramsey)

Richard Dreyfuss (Richard Nelson)

Tagline:

Mayday

Snakes on a Plane (2006)

Plot synopsis

A deadly cargo of venomous snakes is set loose on an aircraft to kill a witness to a gangland murder. FBI agent and other passengers battle the snakes, which kill a number of humans.

Star:

Samuel L. Jackson (Neville Flynn)

Taglines:

Sit back. Relax. Enjoy the fright.

At 30,000 feet, snakes aren't the deadliest thing on this plane.

Airline food ain't what you gotta worry about.

Sunshine (2007)

Plot synopsis:

With the earth under threat from a dying sun a mission is launched to detonate nuclear devices that will re-ignite its power.

Stars:

Cillian Murphy (Capa)

Michelle Yeo (Corazon)

Taglines:

If the sun dies, so do we.

Dark days are coming.

50 years in the future, Earth's Sun is dying.

Doomsday (2008)

Plot synopsis:

Scotland has been quarantined from the rest of Britain by the rebuilding of Hadrian's Wall because of an outbreak of a deadly virus which decimated the population. The virus surfaces in London years later and Major Sinclair tries to find a doctor who was working on the cure before he went missing many years earlier.

Stars:

Rhona Mitra (Maj. Eden Sinclair)

Bob Hoskins (Bill Nelson)

Malcolm McDowell (Marcus Kane)

Taglines:

The End Is Nigh.

Mankind has an expiration date.

Survive This.

Stills information

The publisher believes the following copyright information to be correct at the time of publication, but will be delighted to correct any errors brought to our attention in future editions.

Page 7, *The Towering Inferno* © Warner Bros. / Aquarius Collection; pages 21, 22, 32 and 33, *Airport* © Universal / Joel Finler Archive; page 23, *Grand Hotel* © Aquarius Collection; pages 42, 54 and 55, *The Towering Inferno* © Warner Bros. / Joel Finler Archive; page 43, *The Towering Inferno* © Warner Bros. / Aquarius Collection; page 44, *Jaws* © Universal / Aquarius Collection; page 44, *Star Wars* © 20th Century Fox / Aquarius Collection; pages 67, 69, 70, *The Day After Tomorrow* © 20th Century Fox / Aquarius Collection; page 90, *Cloverfield* © Paramount Pictures / Aquarius Collection; page 91, *Cloverfield* © Paramount Pictures / BFI Stills, Posters & Designs; pages 112, 113, *Airplane!* © Paramount Pictures / Aquarius Collection; page 114, *Airport 1975* and *Airport '77* © Universal / BFI Stills, Posters & Designs; pages 121, 123 and 124, *United 93* © Universal / Aquarius Collection.

The framegrabs which illustrate each 'Textual Analysis' section are taken from the Region 2 DVDs of the respective films.